ENDORSEMENTS

"Church planting is not for the faint of heart. I know because I've done it. So has Kevin Miller, and he's done it successfully. I watched Kevin up close for a number of years as he led youth in our church, and I've observed him as he left to go plant a new church family in Tennessee. The lessons he learned and the principles he shares are priceless. His journey as recorded here can be a lifeline for those like minded but precious few who are willing to go on the adventure."
    Skip Heitzig, Founder and Senior Pastor of Calvary Church in Albuquerque, NM

"Kevin sees the world in a unique and whimsical way that draws you in, engages, and inspires even the most weary heart to rise and see the beauty through the brokenness. His story promises to be a huge statement about the pitfalls and perils of following the calling of the Lord wherever it may lead you, and the inevitable masterpiece we will see in the end. Come Hell or High Water is more than a title... it's something that he's lived, and the story is amazing. Get ready to be inspired."
    Jason Roy, Lead Singer/Songwriter of Building 429

"To be honest, at particular points of this book I had to simply put it down, walk away, and not come back to it for a few days. It was as if Kevin was not just talking to me, but directly about me and my situation working within the four walls of the church. I believe that anyone in ministry or planning on going into the ministry must read this book. It is a field survival manual, hope, reality, encouragement, and a pocket guide to Armageddon all rolled into one. I can relate to being in the unideal church setting where loneliness and criticism were the stereotypical configuration. I faced not only 'lions' (as Kevin calls them) but sheep with very sharp teeth. This book is a healthy reminder that for those of us in the ministry, WE ARE NOT ALONE! There are a lot of us out there who know the truth first hand that 1) God keeps His promises, 2) Satan will attack, and 3) people will let us down.

But that is not the end of the story, or of this book.

Kevin's words rejuvenate the Pastoral spirit and nurture the soul through truth, sincerity, and overwhelming honesty. I highly recommend this book and know it is going to overwhelmingly touch lives and change hearts."

Stephen Christian, Lead Singer/Songwriter of Anberlin, Worship & Creative Director

"Ministry hurts and thrills like no other pursuit on the planet. Kevin Miller insightfully teaches from personal life experience both the highs and lows in an incredibly insightful way. If you are or know a young person in ministry, this book will help them grow."

Luke MacDonald, Associate Pastor at Faithful Central Bible Church in Inglewood, CA

"I have known Kevin Miller for over a decade! His passion to see the local church thrive is unmatched. I believe this book will be an essential tool for anyone who has ever stepped out in faith to do something for Jesus. Kevin has constructed a book on church planting in a manner that is both accurate and practical. Christians at all levels will find this book valuable to them in their personal growth whether they are thinking about, wanting to, or just curious about church planting and the faith that it takes!"

Nate Witiuk, Executive Pastor of Awaken Church in Clarksville, TN

COME HELL OR HIGH WATER

STOPPING AT NOTHING
TO BUILD THE CHURCH

KEVIN MILLER

LifeRich Publishing is a registered trademark of
The Reader's Digest Association, Inc.

LifeRich Publishing books may be ordered through booksellers or by contacting:

LifeRich Publishing
1663 Liberty Drive
Bloomington, IN 47403
www.liferichpublishing.com
1 (888) 238-8637

Because of the dynamic nature of the Internet, any web addresses or
links contained in this book may have changed since publication and
may no longer be valid. The views expressed in this work are solely those
of the author and do not necessarily reflect the views of the publisher,
and the publisher hereby disclaims any responsibility for them.

Any people depicted in stock imagery provided by Getty Images are
models, and such images are being used for illustrative purposes only.
Certain stock imagery © Getty Images.

All emphasis in Scripture references have been added by the author.

"Do It Again" lyrics written by Chris Brown, Mack
Brock, Steven Furtick, and Matt Redman.
Music by Elevation Worship Publishing (BMI) / (admin at
EssentialMusicPublishing.com [3]). All rights reserved. Used by permission.
Copyright © 2016 Thankyou Music (PRS) (adm. worldwide at
CapitolCMGPublishing.com excluding Europe which is adm. by Integrity Music,
part of the David C Cook family. Songs@integritymusic.com) / worshiptogether.
com Songs (ASCAP) sixsteps Music (ASCAP) Said And Done Music (ASCAP)
(adm. at CapitolCMGPublishing.com) All rights reserved. Used by permission.

Cover and interior design: Ellie Tackett
Author photograph: Richard Crozby

ISBN: 978-1-4897-2474-8 (sc)
ISBN: 978-1-4897-2475-5 (hc)
ISBN: 978-1-4897-2482-3 (e)

Library of Congress Control Number: 2019913155

Print information available on the last page.

LifeRich Publishing rev. date: 09/09/2019

TABLE OF CONTENTS

To Jenn,

I'd leave it all behind for you.

INTRODUCTION

*"You may be **SERIOUSLY AND PERMANENTLY INJURED AND/OR KILLED** as a result of your participation. Each participant, regardless of experience has final responsibility for his or her own safety."*

Yeah, yeah, yeah. Give me a pen already so I can sign my life away. My signature on that dotted line was the last thing I needed in order to jump out of an airplane from two and a half miles above the earth. I've ridden in fast cars and been rattled on vomit-inducing roller coasters, but I had never hit terminal velocity while free falling through the sky. The date of my first-ever skydive happened to be the date of my son's third birthday. I couldn't think of a better way to spend his birthday and my Tuesday than in a yellow jumpsuit and goggles, harnessed to a guy I had just met for the first time, falling out of the sky at 120 miles per hour. Tandem skydiving in the morning, Paw Patrol birthday cake at night. Sounds like a good day to me.

We sat in a room and watched a film with epic shots of skydiving jumps as they gave terrible, graphic descriptions of how our bodies could be horribly damaged and/or our lives suddenly ended by skydiving. The video may have scared some people out of it, but not me. The risk and the adventure got me fired up even more.

I guess that's kind of how I'm wired. I like the thrill, the risk, and I easily get bored with monotonous routine.

The first question most people ask me about my skydiving experience was if I was scared. I can honestly say I wasn't. I was so confident in my instructor's ability and the skydiving equipment that I knew I had no need to fear. This wasn't some random group of college guys who started a skydiving company after all. This was the U.S. Army Golden Knights, an elite squad of trained professionals who tour the world tandem jumping out of planes for a living. This is their job! The Golden Knights are to the Army what the Blue Angels are to the Navy. They have done this thousands of times, some of them tens of thousands, with some of the nation's highest ranking officials and well-known celebrities. And also with me.

I had signed the waiver stating I understood the potential risk of severe injury, disfigurement, or death, then turned it in with a smile, promising not to sue the Army if I had to leave the premises in an ambulance, then I put my jumpsuit on and made the heart-pounding walk across the tarmac to the plane. As I ducked through the opening in the side of the airplane, I realized the next time I came through that door, I would be coming out of it. In a freefall.

Each pair of tandem jumpers squeezed into the tiny airplane and off we went. As we climbed into the sky and they yelled final instructions over the noise of the engines, I kept peeking outside as the buildings and cars below got smaller and smaller, eventually becoming almost indistinguishable.

We finally reached jumping altitude. As they flung that door open mid-flight, adrenaline surged through my veins, indelibly marking that moment in my mind. On every other airplane I had ever flown in, it would have been a federal offense to yank open the door. Not this time. Wind whipped through the gaping square of daylight in the side of the plane and the instructor began yelling at each pair of parachuters to begin jumping. The view from 13,000 feet above Clarksville was unreal and the moment my entire day had been building toward had arrived.

"Ready?" My instructor yelled to me over the rush of the wind and whir of the plane's engines. "Let's go!" I yelled back. And with that, my feet left the security of the plane as we began our rapid freefall.

Interestingly, skydiving is a lot like following Jesus in His mission to build the Church. As a church planter, I've experienced this firsthand.

When we moved 1,200 miles across the country to plant a church, I felt about as prepared to plant a church as I felt to skydive after hearing a briefing, watching a training video, and signing a waiver. I didn't know much about either, but I knew enough. I knew it would be challenging. I knew I would be scared at some point. And I knew I had to do it. Now was the time. Come to think of it, the rush of the freefall, the blend of personal loss-of-control and complete trust in my instructor, the intense feelings of excitement mixed with the fear and risk of the unknown... those are all very similar to feelings we've gone through in the years leading up to church planting and in our first decade actually doing it.

The difference is, there's no waiver for planting a church or risking it all as you step out in faith. Planting a church is diving into the unknown. It's plunging into the darkness holding onto the light. It's reaching a community of people with the scandalous message of grace and the foolishness of the cross. The highs are heart-pounding, the lows are backbreaking, and all that you don't know and wish you knew ranges from exhilarating to terrifying. No book, blog, podcast, or college course can ever fully prepare you for the stomach-dropping thrills and spills of parachuting into a community with the gospel, building a team, and leading into the unknown.

Some people think they want God to give them all the details about the future, but I disagree. One of the ways God demonstrates His grace toward us is not by *explaining* the details, but by *sparing* us from them. There are many things we have endured in these first ten years of church planting that could have prevented us from launching out had we known they were coming our way, many of which I will share throughout this book. When it comes to details about the future, you are on a need to know basis. When you need to know, God will let you know!

One of the ways God demonstrates His grace toward us is not by explaining the details, but by sparing us from them.

As thrilling as church planting is and has been, there are plenty of times I have wanted to quit. Recently in one of those hard, I-want-to-quit-and-work-a-nine-to-five-job seasons, when a job as a barista or graphic designer sounded particularly nice, I got a phone call from a pastor friend. He's been in ministry for longer than I've been alive, has planted churches, and has weathered some excruciatingly hard circumstances that would make most people quit. He's one of those people that when you see their name on your phone, you walk out of your meeting or hang up on the other line so you can talk. My calls from him aren't often and they rarely last longer than five minutes (ten would be a long conversation with him), but where our conversations may lack in length, they make up for it in depth and worth. In one of our more recent phone calls, he reminded me of some important truths.

"You know Kevin," he told me, "there are really only about three things that are guaranteed in ministry: 1) God's promises, 2) Satan's attacks, and 3) People letting you down." True, true, and double true. He went on to say, "I can deal with the devil. I expect his attacks. But it's the people that hurt the most. You don't expect it from your closest friends." Then calmly and very matter-of-factly, he said, "Welcome to ministry."

Uh... thanks for the welcome?

I had a long drive home after I hung up from that call, but those words kept ringing in my mind.

The *flood* of people's betrayal.
The *fire* of Satan's attacks.

You can expect both in life, but whether you like it or not, you have front row tickets and backstage passes to them when you're in ministry. It's what you signed up for, even if you don't remember reading that fine print.

I was born in Glendale, Arizona, but grew up in Albuquerque, New Mexico, since the age of three. I started and led my first youth group when I was sixteen and led the Bible club at my high school during my senior year. Right after high school, I did a year of ministry school, then was hired as a middle school Youth Pastor when I was twenty, just four months into marriage. Five years later, my wife Jenn and I and some friends moved across the country to plant Awaken Church when we were in our mid-twenties. As I write this book, we are ten years in. It's been so great, and so hard. There have been some huge mountaintop experiences and some low, dark valleys filled with literal flood waters.

When we moved across the country to plant a church, failure was not an option. We were prepared to stop at nothing to build the church. Come hell or high water, we were ready to do whatever it took to follow the vision and calling God placed on our hearts. We knew it wouldn't be easy, and we were correct.

Jesus said the gates of hell would not prevail against His Church, but we have felt the heat of the flames in this first decade. God led Israel through floodwaters many times and He's done the same with us. I love the way the prophet Isaiah put it:

*"When you go through **deep waters**, I will be with you. When you go through **rivers of difficulty**, you will not drown.*
*When you walk through the **fire of oppression**, you will not be burned up; the flames will not consume you."*
(Isaiah 43:2 NLT)

I didn't write this book to persuade you to plant a church or to argue you out of it. I wrote it to tell a story. A story of God's faithfulness, provision, and gentle prodding. A story of answered prayers despite the doubt that filled them and God's faithfulness even when we were faithless. A story of pain, tragedy, and triumph. It's a powerful story, but it's only the beginning.

I would not call this a how-to book or even a how-not-to book, although I will share plenty of both along the way. This is a story of our experience of the first ten years of planting a church in Clarksville, Tennessee. It's a no-holds-barred look at the behind the scenes of launching out and believing God would use us for something incredible.

Over the years, I have been inspired by so many stories that had very little to do with ministry. I've read the startup stories behind Nike, Google, Amazon, Zappos, Tesla, The Home Depot, and others. I've been inspired by leaders such as Steve Jobs, Louie Zamperini, Elon Musk, and the Wright Brothers. That's not to mention all of the old, dead pastors whose quotes and wisdom have filled the pages of my journals and filled my sails with faith. My story is very different than Steve, Louie, Elon, Orville, and Wilbur, but they inspired me nonetheless. I hope the same is true for you with our story.

In this book, I will be tackling ten of the big lessons we've learned in these first ten years of church planting. Each chapter contains parts and pieces of our story accompanied by lessons learned and practical ways to apply. Our story will not be your story, but I pray our story will inspire yours. You may plant a church some day, or you may preach sermons, plant trees, publish books, purchase homes, paint murals, or a mix of all (or none) of the above. Whatever you do, I hope you're encouraged by our story.

As a final word of encouragement and perspective before we dive in, if you're not a church planter or even on staff at a local church, don't negate your calling to ministry. If you're a Jesus follower, you're a Jesus ambassador. You are chosen, called, empowered, and sent into the world, in whatever context or way you do that. I pray this book gives you a unique peek behind the scenes of ministry, empowers you for your specific calling, and gives you a new perspective on how to support and pray for your pastor. I'm in this with you. Let's change the world together.

Kevin

PART ONE

DON'T JUMP UNTIL YOU'RE READY

PART ONE

ONE
WILLING VS. WIRED

This isn't for everyone.

"Kevin, you have two choices: I can either send you home from camp or I can put you to work. Which will it be?"

"Put me to work, please," I answered as respectfully as possible, inwardly pleading with God not to allow my summer camp mischief to be discovered by my dad and swiftly disciplined out of me.

I'm not sure what I had done to end up in trouble this time, but I imagine it probably had something to do with shaving cream, the girls' bunks, and sneaking out of our dorm room at night. Steve, the Camp Director, rarely had to take such drastic measures with campers. Apparently my pioneer spirit was at work already, charting new territory.

My punishment was that I was to become Steve's shadow. Where Steve went, Kevin went. I fed horses at 5:00am, served meals to campers instead of eating with them, and shoveled horse manure in the afternoon. I hated it all, but I hated the thought of my dad getting a call from the Camp Director even more.

A few years later, I was sixteen and had been attending that summer camp, Lone Tree Bible Ranch, each summer with a small group of church friends for a few years by then. I had been going to summer camps since I was old enough to do so and was accustomed to the "summer camp high." I had ridden that spiritual roller coaster quite a few times by then: go to camp distant from God, come home "changed," let the fire fizzle out quickly and go back to where I had been before, if not worse. Up and down, left and right, tossed around by every swirling emotion and passing feeling.

Something clicked that summer though. I felt different. I don't remember the theme of the teachings, who was speaking, or even what they said, but I know I came home a different guy than when I had left. A few of us did, actually.

We were part of a small church at the time, too small to hire a youth pastor. We didn't want this summer to be simply an upward climb before we took another steep plunge on the spiritual roller coaster, so we made a plan. Five or six of us teenagers sat in a room in the downstairs basement of our bank-turned-church building one Friday night. If they couldn't hire a youth pastor to start a youth group, we would start one ourselves. We could all plan games and get our friends hyped up, but what about the teaching? We would need someone to teach every Friday night. I don't remember the process of selection, but somehow all eyes fell on me.

Thus began my "career" in ministry. We saw a need no one was filling and decided to meet it ourselves. At the ripe old age of sixteen, my role included:

teaching weekly, planning events, and overseeing volunteers.

I had no idea what I was doing and often wanted to quit, but something kept me going.

Fast forward two years to the end of my junior year at Sandia High School. My friends and I would periodically head to the lunchtime Bible Club that met in the choir room each Wednesday. Normally we only went if they were serving pizza, but this particular day, although the pizza was absent, we were present. We sat on the cold, hard, metal bleachers as they nominated club officials for the next school year. As a joke, my friend nominated me to be President of the Bible Club. I couldn't believe my ears and she couldn't contain her laughter.

Apparently curiosity (or the Godfather's Pizza and Dad's Root Beer) got the best of us and we were back the following week to hear who got elected.

"And the President of the Bible Club for the 2001-2002 school year is Kevin Miller!" I almost choked on a pepperoni as everyone cheered for the new President, again, all eyes falling on me.

Me? President of the Bible Club? I barely even attended it, but even my meager attendance eclipsed my desire for the presidency.

This felt like deja vu. Here I was again being "voluntold" to take a ministry leadership position. And for some reason, I did it. That summer, I met with the Vice President, Secretary, and Treasurer of the Bible Club a couple times as we prepared for the upcoming school year. We rebranded the club, giving it the super edgy name *"Souled Out"* (see what I did there?) and geared up for launch, which was just a couple months away.

School started and Souled Out filled up the classroom, forcing us to move out of Mr. Gunther's math classroom into the hallway for the rest of the school year. In addition to leading our youth group on Friday nights, maybe you can guess what I added to my plate every Wednesday. That's right, I was:

teaching weekly, planning events, and overseeing volunteers.

That familiar feeling was back. I had no idea what I was doing and often wanted to quit, but something kept me going.

A year later, I graduated high school and felt compelled to bypass The Lottery Scholarship and opt for a year of ministry school instead. It didn't seem logical, but I knew it was right. That year of ministry school eventually opened the door for me to teach weekly at the middle school youth group at Calvary Church, the largest church in New Mexico and one of the largest in the United States. A teaching gig led to a job offer, and before I knew it, I was a middle school Youth Pastor. I had three main roles as a Youth Pastor:

teaching weekly, planning events, and overseeing volunteers.

Suddenly all those frustrating years of volunteer ministry work came into focus. Those weren't trials; they were training. They weren't meant to break me; God was using them to build me into the leader He wanted me to be.

It turns out my willingness to serve helped me discover what God had wired me to do.

God had spent years working behind the scenes to fuel my heart for ministry. Only a few years into my role as a youth pastor, He began funding my next step in ministry before I even knew where to step.

GOD WILL PEI (THE) WEI

"Kevin, can I come over to your office? I need to talk to you about something." The lady on the other end of the line (we'll call her Lacy and her husband Jerry) worked across the campus from me at the church where I was youth pastor. Her sixth grade son was in my youth group and Jenn and I knew her and her husband fairly well.

Within the next few minutes, she was in my office and an envelope with $500 cash was on the desk between us. "Jerry and I have been praying for you and Jenn and for some reason, we believe we are supposed to give you this money. We feel so strongly about it that if we were to not give you this money, we would be disobeying God."

"You better give me that money then!" I said with a quizzical laugh.

She slid the money across the desk, which felt a little like some sort of mafia drug deal, then we naturally switched to small talk. The kids, work, weather, then she left. She walked out, and I was $500 richer.

That night when I got home from work, I handed the envelope to Jenn and told her about my conversation with Lacy. Jenn was as stunned as I had been all day.

What would you do if someone handed you an envelope with $500 cash that God told them to give to you? The obvious choice for us was dinner out. Nothing extravagant. I think it was Mongolian beef and honey-seared chicken from Pei Wei. Don't judge us. The Lord is the giver of all good gifts, especially Chinese food. The remaining $473.29 went into savings.

Over the next year or year and a half, every four to six weeks, Lacy would swing by my office, hand me an envelope with cash in it, ask about my family, and leave me standing with an amazed look on my face. Sometimes it was $200, sometimes it was $500, but it went on for months. Although I didn't know exactly what was happening, their obedience and generosity was bringing God's plan into focus. The envelopes were part of God's whispers. We were about three years into leading the youth group at this point, and now God was preparing us and providing for something. We just weren't sure what yet.

ASK AND KEEP ASKING

Church planting wasn't always on our radar. Honestly, when I became a youth pastor at the ripe old age of twenty, I don't think I had even given any thought to how churches came into existence. I guess I had never had "the talk" about churches. You know what I mean. The "where do babies come from" talk, but with churches. I guess, like my kids who had no idea how mom suddenly got a baby inside of her, I naively thought churches just appeared one day, and maybe a stork was involved somehow. "You see, when a daddy church loves a mommy church..."

However, in my early twenties, church planting started to make a name for itself. The organic, hippie style of church planting prevalent in the seventies turned much more strategic by the nineties and early 2000s. I began asking questions and hearing stories about how churches got started years, decades, and centuries in the past, and I witnessed from afar as a friend of mine planted and as other friends tried and failed.

Even when God planted the idea in my heart, it took a little while to win my wife over. I remember her asking me, "Plant a church? Like start one from scratch? Wouldn't it be better to just take over a church that already exists that needs a pastor?" If you're married to someone who is not too keen on following you into the great unknown, I hope this is an encouragement to you. My biggest supporter and sidekick didn't even want to do this originally. If that's you, one of two things will happen: 1) God will change their heart eventually like He did my wife's, or 2) God will use their lack of desire to change your direction. After all, unless you're both called and committed to it, don't try it. That won't end well for either of you. Trust me, I've seen it.

The calling to plant a church didn't come in booming-voice-from-heaven form like I wish. Our calling was a lot like Elijah's experience in 1 Kings 19, after his triumph on Mt. Carmel. God wasn't in the earthquake or the fierce wind or the raging fire. He spoke in a still, small voice. But for God, a whisper is all it takes. As we listened over months and years, His whispers began to form the story that would become a future church.

My goal is to live with what I call "Psalm 32 faith."

> **"I will instruct you and teach you in the way you should go**
> **I will guide you with My eye. Do not be like the horse or like the mule,**

Which have no understanding,
Which must be harnessed with bit and bridle,
Else they will not come near you."
(Psalm 32:8–9 NKJV)

If you've been married for a little while, you know your spouse's ability to communicate with you through a glance with their eyes. "Let's get out of here" or "Did you really just say that?" or "Don't you dare" can be communicated and felt with a simple batting of lashes or dart of the eyes. That level of communication can only happen when you know someone really well. That's how attentive I want to be with the Lord. I want to know Him so well and be so attentive to His leading that all it takes is a glance from Him and I know where to go and what to do. After all, I don't want to go the route of the horse or mule who need a bit and bridle because they lack understanding. I lived enough of my life that way. I prefer the former over the latter.

No booming voice. No violent earthquake. No miraculous sign. Just whispers. The best way I can describe His whispers is as a stirring feeling we felt in our hearts. I don't know how else to describe it. We loved our city. We loved our church. We loved our friends and family. We loved authentic New Mexican sopapillas and enchiladas. We were well-connected, well-paid (I got a raise five months before we moved), and we were loving life, but something was stirring. We knew something new was on the horizon; we just didn't know what or why. So we began praying consistently and as specifically as we knew how.

The only way you'll ever know what God wants you to do is to ask and keep asking. Something amazing happens when you consistently pray about something. God will not only speak to you, but He'll begin to speak to others about the same topic and He'll open your eyes to notice and receive His answers. Prayer is preparation for the answer. God always answers prayer, just not always in the ways we expect or want. Remember, "No," "Wait," "Not now," and "Just trust Me" are answers, too. Thankfully, the more you pray, the more you'll listen and be prepared for the answer.

Prayer is preparation for the answer.

THE "FREE TEST"

I was suddenly being awoken from a deep sleep as my body felt itself beginning to fall backwards. It was a violent jolt that jerked me vertical and immediately forced my eyes open.

I had fallen asleep studying again. Thankfully I caught myself this time before I toppled over backwards in my black leather office chair.

It was 1:13 am and I was only partly done with the message I would be teaching at the middle school youth group about eighteen hours later.

I wasn't teaching the youth group because I had extra time to kill. I was in School of Ministry in the mornings and working at an auction house in the afternoons. On top of school and work, I was also planning a wedding. More accurately, I was agreeing with all of the things my fiancée was planning for our wedding. Life was busy and I didn't have extra time. Although my time was limited, I couldn't resist the opportunity that was in front of me. I was compelled; pushed forward by an invisible force. I was stirred up, excited, and willing to what I needed to do so I could do what I was wired to do.

Sometimes people ask me how I knew what my "calling" in life is. I think it's pretty simple to figure out, actually. I call it the "free test." A tell tale sign of a calling is what you are willing to do for free. When you fall asleep doing it, wake up thinking about it, and constantly try to figure out how you can do more of it, either you have an unhealthy obsession or a God-given calling.

> When you fall asleep doing it, wake up thinking about it, and constantly try to figure out how you can do more of it, either you have an unhealthy obsession or a God-given calling.

As I look back, I realize that since the age of sixteen, I have been finding ways and making time to do what I'm wired to do on top of all the things I have to do.

Another test is if you are able to push past discouragement

and antagonism as you pursue what you believe God has wired you to do. Trust me, there will be plenty of both.

ANTI-PRAYERS

"I'm praying *against* you planting a church."

Those were the unexpected words that came out of the mouth of an acquaintance of mine when he found out I planned to plant a church in Clarksville, Tennessee. For obvious reasons, his antagonistic prayer has stuck with me all these years.

To be honest, there have been a couple times where I have been equally discouraging to hopeful church planters.

"You should not plant a church" or "you're not ready" are pieces of actual advice I've told to a couple of wide-eyed young guys ready to set out on the adventure of their lifetime. Although I've rarely given that advice, it is the truth for most people.

Ninety-nine percent of people should not plant churches. Just as a career in oral surgery or college-level trigonometry are not for most, church planting is not for most.

Biblically, all Christians are ministers of the gospel, whether they're on staff at a church or not.

A few Christians are called to pastor others.

A few pastors are called to plant churches.

Unless you are in that final small group, my advice stands firm. You should not plant a church. As Charles Spurgeon said in *Lectures To My Students*, "If any student in this room could be content to be a newspaper editor or a grocer or a farmer or a doctor or a lawyer or a senator or a king, in the name of heaven and earth, let him go his way..."[1] His point is that if you could find fulfillment in any other career path or calling, you are not called to pastor a church, or in our case, plant a church. A calling to do something besides pastoring isn't a bad thing at all. In fact, it's still a calling and you should treat it as such.

His point is following fulfillment. The reality is, if you're following anything else than where fulfillment is at its greatest, you'll be miserable. Fulfillment doesn't come simply because you are doing something you are *willing* to do; fulfillment comes when you are doing what you are *wired* to do. You can be content wherever you are, but you'll only be fulfilled when you're where God has wired you to be.

> Fulfillment doesn't come simply because you are doing something you are willing to do; fulfillment comes when you are doing what you are wired to do.

I'm not trying to discourage people from planting churches. We need more churches to be planted now than ever before. However, the reality is that if a seemingly disparaging statement can dissuade someone from planting, then obviously they're not called to it to begin with. If you can't push past an antagonistic comment, you'll never survive in the cutthroat world of differing opinions, ever-changing preferences, and Christian consumerism that is so prevalent in the modern American church. If you can't handle some heavy criticism, not only are pastoring and planting not for you, but you'll be miserable if you attempt them. Criticism and opinions abound, trust me.

Let me break it down a little further.

GO GET A HOBBY

Church planting is not just something fun to do. It's not cool. It's not a hobby. It's not something you should do because you're "looking for a new challenge" or you "haven't tried that yet." People celebrate their birthdays by jumping out of airplanes because it's a rush, but then you walk away and eat dinner with your family that night and go on with your life. If you are simply wanting to try something new, Wikipedia has a great article called "List of hobbies"[2] that may be helpful. "3D Printing," "Meme Fact Checking," "Bus spotting," and "Rock balancing" are just a few examples of some things you may find interesting and entertaining.

If you're bored or want a new challenge, go spot a bus or balance some rocks; don't plant a church.

I'm not trying to be negative about church planting. I'm trying to be realistic. I don't think there's enough of that these days. Here's the cold, hard truth: had my wife Jenn and I not known for sure that we were called to plant a church in Clarksville, TN, we would have packed our bags and quit in year one. Maybe in month one when a visitor to our church told me I was a chore to listen to or in month three when most of our church deployed except the ladies and children or in month eight when we lost everything in a flood. You get the point. We are doing what we are doing not just because we are willing, but because we were wired to do this. It wasn't just a good idea for us to plant a church; this was God's idea.

Don't get me wrong. I love what I do. I can't imagine doing anything else. But the main reason I love it is because I know I'm doing exactly what I'm supposed to do where I'm supposed to do it. The only way church planting or stepping out in faith in any area will ever be fun or rewarding is if you're called to it. Even the most difficult callings have invaluable rewards when you know you are doing what God wired you to do.

For us, church planting has rarely been easy, but if easy was what I was after, I wouldn't live in Clarksville and I wouldn't be writing this book. I also wouldn't have kids and I may not have gotten out of bed this morning.

MAKING SENSE IS OVERRATED

Rarely is a calling from God easy or logical. Faith, by definition, is illogical. The author of Hebrews defines faith as "the evidence of things we cannot see" (Hebrews 11:1 NLT). What?! If the evidence can't be seen, how can it be considered evidence? A police investigator who brings in a bag of unseen evidence will lose his job pretty quickly. How is this even logical? It's not. And that's kind of the point when it comes to faith.

Before we go further, let me be clear. Faith in God, although not logical by dictionary definition, is not moronic or blind, as some say. It's the only natural response when we look around at creation (Romans 1:20 ESV) and at the evidence of His grace and provision. Honestly, it takes far more faith to believe we all accidentally evolved over millions of years than to believe we were created, but that is probably a discussion for an apologetics book, not a ministry book.

Here's where I'm going with this... The calling that God has on your life won't make sense to some people, yourself included. That's certainly been the story of my life and journey in following Jesus so far. It wasn't logical for me to be selected to run my youth group at the age of sixteen, lead my high school Bible Club that

I had rarely attended, or bypass a scholarship and go to ministry school instead of an accredited college. And I agree. It wasn't logical. But I wasn't attempting to follow logic. I was following God's leading. I was following an inward pull. I couldn't see it, describe it, or escape it.

I mean, I guess I could have escaped it. I could have resisted and run the other way. But that's what I had spent years of my life doing. I had been Jonah on the ship to Tarshish for too long. This time, it was different. I knew advertising design school wasn't for me and ministry school was. In hindsight, it makes sense. In regular sight (or whatever the opposite of hindsight is), it didn't make sense. My parents and I felt hesitant. But now I'm learning that following a calling is often accompanied by hesitancy, doubt, and an endless list of what ifs.

And by the way, the faith God was teaching me in my teens was building a foundation for the future: I would need it at twenty-three as we explored a cross-country move, at twenty-five when we sold our house and car and left everything we knew behind, at twenty-six when a flood destroyed the building our eight-month old church met in, at twenty-seven and twenty-eight when Jenn miscarried, and many more times since then.

Here's my point...

Following God into the unknown is the best, most wild, and fruitful life you can live. I remember all those "how" questions that filled our minds early on...

How would we make the move?

How would we do this thing we'd never done?

How would we pay for this crazy endeavor?

Through trial and error, God is teaching me that I don't have to know *how* when I know *Who*. In fact, when I know *Who*, *how* becomes a minor detail I let Him figure out. Every step of faith you take is worth the risk because even when you don't know the future, you serve the God who holds it. Who over how every day. If you keep waiting to follow God until He maps out all the details like Google Maps, you'll miss out on the adventure of the journey. Embrace the detours, the dips, the delays, and the distance. It's all part of it, and they'll make you better prepared when you arrive.

I don't have to know how when I know
Who.

When God commands something, He equips, empowers, and enables you to accomplish it. If He is for you, it doesn't matter who or what is against you. Don't pull a Jonah and run from your calling. If God could use a rebellious, reluctant prophet who smelled like fish vomit to bring about the largest revival in recorded human history, imagine what He can do with someone who is willing and ready to do what He says! After all, the church isn't yours anyway. Jesus said He would build *His* church. We just get to be part of it for a few years.

When God commands something, He equips, empowers, and enables you to accomplish it. If He is for you, it doesn't matter who or what is against you.

The calling God has on your life won't always make sense, and neither will the steps of faith God calls you to take along the way. People thought we were crazy when two hundred people from our church marched around an empty 90,000-square-foot Kmart building in thirty-nine degrees and blowing rain (more on that later). People thought we were crazy for adding a video venue on the same campus under the same roof as our current venue. People thought we were crazy when we gave all the money that came in on Easter away to our ministry partners instead of saving for our buildout project.

Crazy? Probably. Called? Absolutely.

Speaking of logic, let me remind you of Paul's words to the Corinthians. Referencing their calling, he writes:

"For consider your calling, brothers: not many of you were wise according to worldly standards, not many were powerful, not many were of noble birth. But God chose what is foolish in the world to shame the wise;

God chose what is weak in the world to shame the strong; God chose what is low and despised in the world, even things that are not, to bring to nothing things that are, so that no human being might boast in the presence of God."
(1 Corinthians 1:26–29 ESV)

Like the Corinthians' calling to ministry, yours and mine are also illogical. According to "worldly standards," things won't always line up. God purposely chooses to use unexpected things, people, and methods so He is the one who gets all the credit. The sooner you learn to be ok with that, the more fruitful your ministry and life will be.

I am not saying do stupid things in the name of Jesus. In fact, please don't. Plenty of people are already doing that. Just read the news over the next few weeks and you'll probably hear something about a robbery or drug deal or streaking incident that was done "because God told them to." Right. Sure He did. Here, try this straight jacket on for size.

CROSS-COUNTRY PRAYERS

I'll tell you more in the next chapter about how we landed on Clarksville, but for now, let me pull back the curtain on some of the prayer that was taking place behind the scenes. I wrote earlier about continually asking God for direction and timing, and that's what we did. Not only were we praying for years before we had even heard of Clarksville, we continued praying for God's timing once we knew the location. Not only did we want to go to the right place, but also at the right time. For months, we prayed God would send the right person to fill my role as youth pastor and that God would clarify when the right time was for us to leave and launch.

Then came Saturday night, October 16.

I was teaching the youth group that night at church and Jenn was at home with a sick kid. After service was over, I talked with friends as people slowly trickled out of the church building, heading out to dinner or home for the evening. I ended up talking with a pastor who had recently moved from Tennessee back to Albuquerque, and he told me all about the area and the need for good Bible-teaching churches. As we talked, I felt an overwhelming urgency to launch out that I had not felt before. It felt all-consuming. Like we had to do it. I drove home, walked in the door, and told

Jenn, "We have to pick a date to move to Clarksville. There will be a hundred reasons for us to stay. God has given us a place and it's time to pick a date and make it happen."

Fast forward four months. May 2009 is our move date. We'll be in Clarksville June 2009. In February, we took our final scouting trip. We wanted to look for houses, jobs, and meet with some local pastors. One of the pastors we met with has a church in Goodlettsville, TN, about forty-five minutes from Clarksville. We toured his church, shared our vision, and prayed together with him. As he walked us out, he said, "You know, it's really great that you're here. We just had a pastors conference back in October and we specifically prayed that God would bring a pastor to plant a church in Clarksville. We are so glad you're here!" Those were such encouraging words to hear as we walked out the door that day to head back to Clarksville.

Finding out you are the answer to someone's prayer is encouraging enough, but as we drove out of their parking lot, it hit us. He mentioned their conference was last October. Out of curiosity, I called him back. "What was the date of that pastors' conference you mentioned?" I asked him. "Uhhh. Let me think... It was Saturday, October 16," he replied. If only he could have seen the awe on my face on the other end of the phone line. As tears welled up in my eyes, I hung up the phone with an even greater sense of confirmation and direction.

Little did those pastors know that as they prayed that night, God was immediately and directly answering their prayers 1,235 miles across the United States in a city most of them had never been to in the heart of a young pastor they had never met. Little did I know that the overwhelming feeling I had that night was what it felt like when God is specifically directing the course of your life through the faith-filled prayers of other people.

I needed things like this. In fact, I had asked God often for them. Like Gideon needed confirmation on a fleece, I needed to know that quitting my job (a scary, seemingly illogical thing to do) and planting a church (something I had never done and barely even seen done) in Clarksville, TN (a city 1,200 miles away that I had never lived in and where we knew no one) was God's idea and not my own. I'm a pioneer. I think if I wasn't in full time ministry, I'd probably be an entrepreneur/business owner. With that mentality in my bloodstream, I didn't want to risk the potential of moving across the nation fueled by my next good idea. I had to know this was a God idea. As Jenn and I asked and kept asking for years, God continued to confirm that calling.

FAMILY FUNERALS

"I'm in my final year of morgue school," Presleigh told me. She was the nineteen-year-old daughter of the owner of the funeral home I was at. I was meeting with her as I prepared to do the funeral for the father of one of my friends, who had just lost his battle with cancer. Presleigh was following in a long line of footsteps as her family had made death their life's business and ministry for multiple generations. Doing funerals is hard enough for me; I can't imagine doing them as a business every day! I talked to her about the funeral service I'd be doing as well as about her role in the funeral home. In my short interaction with her, I was reminded that everyone everywhere has a calling. Church planter or cello player, choir director or chiropractor, business owner or bus driver, pharmacist or farmer, everyone has something God has wired them to do (see Ephesians 2:10). Although I'd be *willing* to do a lot of things, there are only a few things I'm *wired* to do. Presleigh plans funerals. I plant and pastor churches. Neither is better or worse, good or bad; they're just different. Different is necessary and good.

You be you. Don't try to be me or anyone else. Comparison will sabotage your calling and suck the joy out of life. Not only is your calling unique, but how God calls you will be unique. Don't wait for a lady to bring you envelopes of cash so you'll know you're called. Don't expect a pastors conference to happen where their prayers for you are answered immediately. And as I'll share later, don't do some of the things we did early on. I think God spoke to me most often through sermons because that's a primary way I speak. I know and live for the power of God's Word, so God often speaks to me in that same way. Similarly, God often speaks in a language you understand because He is that personal of a God. One of my best friends writes and records songs for a living, so God regularly uses that medium to get his attention. If you will just be faithful to hit pause and listen, God will be faithful to speak. He promises to do so.

Remember the advice I shared earlier in this chapter, "You should not plant a church?" I haven't always felt the liberty to tell that to people I felt were making a mistake going out to plant, but

I've considered it. If through prayer and reading this book, you come to the conclusion that you were not supposed to plant a church, that would be a great thing. Not because we don't need more churches, but because we need more people functioning in their calling and gifting, not in someone else's. I've seen a few guys go out to plant churches who seem to assume that's just the next step in their "career path" of ministry or something. The way God has built you helps determines what He has called you to do and how He is calling you to do it.

99

You be you. Don't try to be me or
anyone else. Comparison will sabotage
your calling and suck the joy out of life.

So don't plant a church...unless you *can't not* plant a church. Then go do it and give it your all. Surround yourself with great, Godly examples, learn from the best of the best, read books, study hard, pray harder, then take that step of faith God is leading you toward. Lead that church like it's the only one you'll ever lead because it very well may be!

Now if only you knew where to go. Let's talk about that next.

TWO
OPERATION: LOCATION DETERMINATION

If you will follow, He will lead.

Jenn and I are slightly obsessive over where we eat. Whenever we travel, be that heading east on I-24 to Nashville or across the U.S. in Portland, we take great care in finding a local eatery with great Yelp reviews and preferably no more than two dollar signs, three max. I'm not proud of it, but we've been known to spend forty-five minutes sitting on a hotel bed scouring Yelp for the best of the best or arguing about whether the outdoor seating on the Yelp review looks up to our standards or not. We had some friends who traveled to Manhattan for their anniversary. He happened to be fasting from coffee at the time (have you ever even heard of that?) and since there was a Starbucks in the lobby of their hotel, that's the only coffee shop they went to while they were there. I was sad for them that they were in the land of Blue Bottle and Intelligentsia, but only went to *Starbucks!* Gasp! The horror!

Yeah, we're *those* people.

If finding a local place to eat is worth that much effort, then surely the location of your future church plant or faith venture is worth more work than flipping a coin, rolling some dice, or throwing a dart at a map. And don't just let cash be your compass. If your only purpose is a paycheck, you should think twice about going. I know God can and will use us any time, anywhere, in any way, but seeking Him about where to go is really important.

According to the United States Geological Survey [1], there are over 35,000 cities and towns in the U.S. That's 35,000 locations for you to choose from to plant a church...and those are just *cities and towns in the United States.* You could also plant a church anywhere around the world or in the forest or jungle somewhere (not recommended). In other words, you literally have endless options for where to plant a church.

Or do you?

Will God bless you *wherever* you go?

The answer to that question probably depends on who you ask.

Based on God's specific plans and extreme attention to detail demonstrated throughout Scripture, I tend to lean toward the belief that God has somewhere specific He wants to send you. Sure, God is with you wherever you are, but if He cared about the measurements of the Ark of the Covenant down to the inch and the exact order and color of the High Priest's clothing in Exodus, I have a hard time believing He would be flippant and random with something as important as His bride — the Church — the one thing He left in our hands and promised to build Himself.

FROM THE 505 TO THE 931

"Clarksville? Where's that?"

When we told people we were moving to Clarksville, TN, most people only knew Clarksville from the 1966 Monkees song, *Last Train To Clarksville*. Fun fact: there is actual footage of Clarksville in the music video on YouTube, including a shot of the bridge that runs right in front of our church to this day. And no, we didn't take a train to Clarksville, but thanks for asking. My wife and daughter took a plane, and my dad and I took a moving truck that broke down at mile marker 207 on I-40 East outside of Oklahoma City. If you're ever in the area, take a selfie with the mile marker and thank God you're not there with a broken down moving truck with a wasp nest in its door...yeah, that happened.

Once I run through the normal explanation about our location: "It's about forty-five minutes northwest of Nashville on the Kentucky-Tennessee border," the next question is, "Why?"

It's a good question. Why move somewhere where we didn't know anyone to do something we'd never done in a city most people have never heard of? Let's just say Clarksville wasn't our first choice.

A.S.A.P. / A.L.A.T.

In his book, *Chase the Lion* [2], author and pastor Mark Batterson talks about persistence in prayer. He says we are accustomed to praying A.S.A.P. prayers (As Soon As Possible), but we should be more focused on praying A.L.A.T. prayers (As Long As it Takes).

When it comes to church planting and following Jesus in general, be forewarned that the prayer process will take you longer than you want it to. The good news is, it will also prepare you more than you thought you needed.

Insider hint: praying about this is less about the destination and more about the preparation. So often we pray about the work of ministry and forget that prayer is the work. Stay committed to praying as long as it takes and you won't be able to keep up with what God does.

Praying about this is less about the destination and more about the preparation.

I speak from experience on this. I mentioned earlier that it took Jenn a little while to come around to the idea of planting a church. Taking over an already existing church? She was down with that. Starting from scratch, like putting a seed in the ground, and nurturing it into growth? Not so much. At least that was her take at first. But the pause is ok. I'm learning that the delay is a necessary part of the preparation. Had we prayed a couple times and leapt, we would have fallen flat on our faces, as I have seen others do.

Not only will the prayer process take longer than you want it to, but if you're like me, you will also question the whole thing along the way. More than a few times, probably. That's ok. Questions and doubt are part of the game. It's called being human. Don't beat yourself up for it. Just keep talking to God. If you're only praying so you can get an answer, you're missing out on the most important part of prayer: getting to know God more. We don't just talk to God to get the answer; He is the Answer!

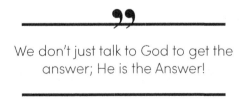

We don't just talk to God to get the answer; He is the Answer!

Unlike your mom who eventually snapped at you for asking so many questions when you were young, God loves it when we keep asking. In fact, Jesus told a story in Luke 18 for the entire purpose of teaching the disciples to pray and not lose heart. God is not annoyed by your incessant questioning and He's not concerned by your up and down struggle with doubting. He just wants to talk about all of it so He can teach you how trustworthy He is through the struggle.

I met a guy in our church a couple years ago after he was diagnosed a second time with cancer. That week I was studying Luke 1, the text I'd be teaching week one of our Christmas series from. As I studied, Luke 1:14 jumped out at me. It's an angelic prophecy given to Zechariah, but as I studied it, I had the distinct impression it was also for someone who would hear the message I was preparing. That Sunday a friend of mine introduced me to Terry and asked me to pray for his healing. As I prayed for him, I felt led to speak that prophecy to him. As we prayed, I quoted it, "And you will have joy and gladness, and many will rejoice..." It was a powerful, gripping moment as the Holy Spirit moved. I told Terry to find me every Sunday he could make it to church and I would pray for him. I just knew God was going to do something miraculous.

I've been praying for Terry for going on two years now. He's at church almost every Sunday. Sometimes he feels and looks great. Other times, he is weak, pale faced, and actively hooked up to his chemotherapy medication while he sits there listening to the message, trying to hold down the little he has in his stomach.

I honestly didn't think we would be praying this long. I thought the miracle would take place quicker. It turns out, I was looking for the wrong miracle. Although God hasn't fully healed Terry's cancer yet, He has transformed his heart. After all, who cares if you are cancer-free if you are lugging around a hardened heart? Like the lame man lowered through the roof who Jesus forgave before He healed him, Jesus is changing Terry spiritually as He changes him physically.

He has made some great strides toward the end of his cancer and is feeling progressively better week by week and month by month. I told him we will pray A.L.A.T.

As God is changing Terry, God is also changing me. He's reminding me to trust Him even when the answer looks different and takes longer than I expected.

BLURRY SIGHT AND GROWING FAITH

I started my second grade year with my first pair of glasses, so much of my life has been lived with the struggle of not always being able to see clearly. Some of my more frustrating reminders of my nearsightedness happen when Jenn cleans our bathroom counter off, neatly placing into drawers the things I had conveniently left on the counters. When I take my contacts out without realizing my glasses aren't in the convenient spot I always leave them in, I am momentarily handicapped as I fumble around through a blurry mess of unidentifiable objects until I feel what seems to be my glasses. As I finally find them and put them on, all the things I could barely see come into focus.

Sight is an incredible blessing that those of us with it easily take for granted. But here's a crazy thought: what if you are allowing the God-given gift of sight to hinder your faith?

So much of our faith journey has been stepping out when we didn't have a lot of clear direction. Like me fumbling through the drawers in search of my glasses, following Jesus sometimes feels out of focus and slightly disorienting. I am still learning there will be a lot that I can't see, but that should not stop me from stepping.

After about a year or so praying about what this next leap of faith would look like, we didn't know much, but at least three things started coming into focus:

1) Church planting was our next step. Not youth ministry. Not taking over another church. Leading a church we were going to start.

2) It wouldn't be in New Mexico. We loved New Mexico; we just knew our church plant would not be there. It felt like progress to narrow our location search from fifty to forty-nine states.

3) We weren't ready yet. We knew the time wasn't yet, but that it would come. We would walk until God shut a door or redirected us.

As we began praying about where we would go and when, Jenn's dad got a job working for a school system in a little city called Paris, TN. It has an Eiffel Tower, but trust me, it's nothing like the Paris. It was fun telling people Jenn's parents lived in Paris, though.

They were moving to "the Bible Belt," so surely finding a great church would be easy. Right? Not so much. They found the best church they could find, but still really struggled with it. Within a few months of them moving, we were in their home on vacation and at their church on Sunday, realizing the spiritual climate was very different in that part of the United States. After attending a few churches with Jenn's family, we started realizing that "the Bible belt" is much more like the "Religion Ring." There's a lot of religion and tradition, and not nearly enough Bible and Jesus. We saw the need, but still needed a lot of convincing that Tennessee was where we were supposed to go.

We put a high emphasis on going where there was a need. Every city can benefit from another great Bible-teaching church, but I believe extra attention should be focused where you sense there is a great need. Where do you feel drawn? Where could God use you to reach a certain demographic? Which cities do you feel drawn to? Start there.

If that city/neighborhood/people group is on your heart, it's probably there for a reason. God promises to give wisdom when you ask (see James 1:5). From dreams to job interviews, miraculous funding and seemingly coincidental run-ins with people we met as we stepped out in faith, God directed us to Clarksville. I have no doubt He will direct you too, as you pray, listen, take notes, and follow Him into the unknown. But buckle up. It will take longer, be harder, and stretch you further than you realized.

As you search for a city and location, don't discount your personality and desires along the way. God wired you the way He did on purpose. It's no accident that you have a desire to live in certain places and not in others. It goes without saying that we should put God's desire above our own, but also don't assume God is going to automatically make you plant a church somewhere that you hate. Why do we so easily reduce God's will to something so miserable? Surely I'm not the only one who grew up with that skewed mentality, thinking "serving God" meant being a missionary to the slums of Africa. Some are called to that. I am not. I am called to plant and pastor churches. Many are not.

That doesn't mean ministry won't take you to some dangerous places, out of your comfort zone. Faith, by definition, is out of your comfort zone. Throughout the Bible, God took people to some challenging places for ministry, but He also commonly used people and personalities in strategic ways. After all, chances are, you'll be much more successful at reaching people if you live somewhere you enjoy and do what you love.

That's a principle to tuck in your back pocket for later in ministry, too. At Awaken, sometimes people will ask, "Which team should I serve on? Where is the greatest need?" Although I love the servant's heart behind that question, we prefer to go at it from a different angle. Instead of starting with the need in the church, we start with the gift in the person. There's a reason God wired that person with those gifts, desires, and skills, so we try to be strategic with them. Sometimes we need to serve in an area that's uncomfortable or unnatural, and sometimes, at least temporarily, we place someone on a team to fill an immediate need. If you plant a church or serve at a church early on, you will wear plenty of hats. However, serving God isn't meant to be torture. You're His work of art, and He wants to use you to create other works of art! Living out your calling is the most thrilling way to live your life. It's fraught with risk, challenge, and discomfort, but it's the best possible way to live!

99

Living out your calling is the most thrilling way to live your life. It's fraught with risk, challenge, and discomfort, but it's the best possible way to live!

There will be many unknowns throughout the rest of your life and ministry, but especially in the initial phases of prayer and preparation. To anyone seeking to step into the place and position God has designed them for, keep praying and keep stepping. If, at times, it feels like blindly fumbling, get used to that feeling. That's what walking by faith feels like.

L.T.D. (LIVING THE DREAM)

Jenn and I have had some crazy dreams over the years. Jenn once had a dream that she ran into a guy who had deeply hurt a friend of ours. In her sleep, she approached the perpetrator and backhanded him! Fortunately for him and unfortunately for me, he was only there in her dream and I was there in person. Sometime around midnight, in a deep moment of beautiful, restful sleep, I received a sudden, violent blow to my face. She hit me so hard, it knocked me out of bed, onto the floor! I grabbed the night stand and stood up, trying to understand what happened and figure out how to defend myself from this surprise assailant. Somehow, I miraculously escaped bleeding and bruising from that backhand. Lesson learned: don't mess with my wife!

Another time early in our marriage, also deep into my sleep cycle, Jenn sat up suddenly in bed, violently gripping my thigh, yelling, "WHERE ARE THE TUMS?!" As my brain was suddenly awoken, my mind swirled with thoughts about what could be so bad that would cause a need that suddenly. I've had heartburn before, but never that bad! Before I could gain my composure and have the clarity of mind to ask her what was wrong, Jenn slowly laid back down, sound asleep. She had never actually been awake. I, on the other hand, was wide awake. For hours.

Weird dreams are one thing, but God dreams are another. Throughout Scripture, dreams were a common way God spoke to His people. God used dreams and visions to direct and comfort Laban, Joseph, Daniel, Paul, John, and many others. The dream I can relate to most is in Acts 10. Peter falls into a trance waiting on lunch to be prepared. It's reassuring to know I am not the only one who has dozed off dreaming of my next meal! Don't you dare tell me the Bible isn't relevant!

Nate, one of my best friends, and the Executive Pastor at Awaken, hears from God periodically through dreams. When he's tired, we often joke that he should go exercise his spiritual gift!

Dreams had never been a way God communicated to me until we began praying about church planting. At first, the dreams were not ours though.

In 2007, as our family prepared to leave for a Tennessee Christmas vacation, a friend of ours asked if we were moving there to start a church. I was shocked. The thought had crossed my mind, but not the desire. When I asked why she was asking, I was amazed (and slightly scared) to find out she had dreamed about us moving there to do just that! Obviously her revelation changed the tone of our trip. We journeyed with packed bags and wide-open eyes and hearts. And sure enough, as I listened, God spoke.

That Christmas trip to Tennessee, while we stayed with Jenn's family, became one of only a few times in my entire life God has spoken to me through a dream. In the dream, we walked into a YMCA, and my pastor was in the pool about to baptize someone. He called me into the water, and as the person came out of the water, my pastor introduced me to them and said to him, "This is Kevin, your new pastor. He's starting a church in Tennessee!"

So maybe there was something to this idea after all, I thought. We knew we would be back to Tennessee again soon.

GOING BACK TO TN, TN, TN...

We journeyed back to Albuquerque, then two months later, our plane touched down again in Nashville. You can pray about something any time anywhere, but there's something about being on location, or as our military friends call it, "boots on the ground." The trip was worth a few hundred dollars in plane tickets, hotel stays, and meals, as we explored this scary, exciting, full-of-questions stirring we were feeling.

Jenn and I weren't cut out for the podunk city life of Paris, TN, with its knockoff chain restaurants and one shoe store that felt more like a flea market than a legit establishment. So before we made the trip, we researched the bigger cities in Tennessee. We narrowed our sights on three larger cities, and made plans to visit each during our few days in Tennessee.

City #1: Jackson, TN. Population 60,000. We had been there before and enjoyed it. It was growing and had a nice mall and a Starbucks, so it was already a step up from Paris.

City #2: Mt. Juliet, TN. Population 19,000, but rapidly expanding. As one of the newest Nashville suburbs, it showed a lot of promise and was already experiencing a lot of growth.

City #3: Clarksville, TN. Population 120,000. We had never been to Clarksville and still hadn't heard the Monkees song, but the city was intriguing. At the time, Clarksville was considered the fastest growing large city in Tennessee. It had a growing local college and the nation's second largest Army post, Ft. Campbell, which hosts 30,000 soldiers and their families.

We landed in Nashville, drove to Paris — our home base for this quick scouting trip — dropped our daughter with the grandparents, and hit the road for Jackson, sure we were driving into our future home. As we pulled into Jackson, somehow we immediately knew that was not the spot. Jackson is a great city, so I can't put a finger on why we knew it wasn't the place for us. I guess the feeling we had was similar to that feeling you get on the first date when you know this relationship isn't going anywhere. Don't take it personally, Jacksonians; it's not you, it's us. We had planned to stay there that night, but changed our minds and our plans, booked a room at the MicroTel in Clarksville (our hotel tastes have greatly improved since then), and drove there instead.

There was something about Clarksville. We couldn't put a finger on it and we didn't know exactly what we were looking for, but we felt drawn to this city. As we drove into the heart of the city under the cover of darkness, our stomachs led us to dinner at Rafferty's on the main strip. I can still show you the exact table we sat at. I remember ordering our meal, then looking across the table at Jenn, thinking "What are we doing here?" Only our nearest family members knew we were there. Even our friends and employers back home had no idea. They just thought it was a quick weekend getaway. We enjoyed our meals, drove around the city a bit, then called it a night, anxious to see the city in the daylight.

The next day, we aimlessly wandered around the city, taking in the sights as we drove, wondering what we were doing and why we were even there.

Would there be a booming voice from heaven or some clear sign that we had found the right city?

Was this a spiritual game of hot and cold?

How would we know if this was the place we were supposed to be?

If God had been funding this move for the past few months, surely He had a specific place He wanted us to go. Was Clarksville it?

After aimlessly driving around the city for half of the day, intermittently praying, stopping to see sights and explore churches, we decided to investigate the housing. After all, if this was where we were going to live, we'd need a house. We remembered passing a real estate kiosk in the mall the night before, so we made that our next stop. We walked into the mall through the outdated JCPenney and up to the kiosk. Apparently we had arrived at lunch break, so the kiosk had as many realtors as we had answers: none.

There we stood confused, lost, wondering what we were supposed to do, trying to explore this idea we had with no real clue how to explore. As we stood there in the middle of a strange mall in a city we didn't know, an elderly man walked up to us and said, "You look lost. Can I point you in the right direction?" I explained to him that we were thinking about moving to Clarksville to plant a church and needed info about housing, but didn't know who to talk to or where to go. You should have seen the look on his face! Then out of his mouth came tumbling the first of many confirmations we needed and God so graciously provided.

"You're here to do what?" he exclaimed, shocked.

"We are thinking about planting a church here in Clarksville, so we need to find out some information about the local real estate," I replied.

"My name is Verlon Moore," he said, excitedly extending his hand toward mine. "You probably won't believe me when I say this, but I'm a retired Southern Baptist preacher. I just got my real estate license a year ago, and my favorite thing to do is help pastors find houses and church buildings!"

I couldn't believe what I was hearing. He called his wife over to join us, and there, in the middle of Governor's Square Mall, by an empty bench outside of Victoria's Secret, we held hands with a couple about three times our age as they prayed for God to guide our search for a home and a church building.

As he closed the prayer with a hearty Baptist "amen," he said, "If you want to jump in your car and follow me, I'll show you around town." Of course we did! We had walked into the mall fifteen minutes ago feeling aimless and lost, and now we were walking out with our new best friend, Brother Verlon Moore, our retired-preacher-turned-real-estate-agent-and-angel friend, guiding us around town. Within minutes, we were touring the city, looking at houses, convinced we were in the right place.

It's amazing what can happen when you pray and take a step of faith.

It's amazing what can happen when
you pray and take a step of faith.

Suddenly the "no" we felt about planting in Albuquerque, Jackson, and everywhere else we had entertained so far, made a lot more sense. God was using every "no" to get us go to where He really wanted us.

NO MEANS GO

I once heard someone say, "When you can't see far, go as far as you can see." You may not know the timing or destination just yet, but you can at least plan a weekend trip (to the aforementioned city/neighborhood/people group) with your spouse or some friends, and attend a church or two and pray. If nothing else, you got a weekend trip out of it, and checked a potential location off your list. That's worth an airline ticket and a hotel!

And if as you step out, you are met with a big "NO," don't stress; you're in good company. The same thing happened to the greatest, most prolific church planter of all time, Paul the Apostle. In Acts 16, as Paul desperately attempted to share the gospel with as many people as possible, he unsuccessfully attempts multiple times to share the gospel in Asia. Interestingly, it isn't Satanic oppression that shuts him down, it's God! Acts 16:6 and 7 contain some of the most perplexing verses in his church planting journey:

> **"And they went through the region of Phrygia and Galatia, having been forbidden by the Holy Spirit to speak the word in Asia. And when they had come up to Mysia, they attempted to go into Bithynia but the Spirit of Jesus did not allow them."**
> **(Acts 16:6-7 ESV)**

God Himself prevented Paul the Apostle from preaching and planting! Can you imagine how frustrating that must have been for Paul? He was getting after it, doing what he knew God had called, prepared, commanded, and empowered him to do. Then God Himself inexplicably stood in his way. Thankfully Paul didn't give up or resign from ministry at this juncture. He learned a valuable lesson as he kept praying. It turns out God wasn't saying NO as much as He was saying GO. As Paul sought God's direction, he had a vision of a man calling for help from Macedonia. Then he did something so wild, I have a hard time wrapping my mind around it.

> **"And when Paul had seen the vision, immediately we sought to go on into Macedonia, concluding that God had called us to preach the gospel to them."**
> **(Acts 16:10 ESV)**

I want Acts 16:10 faith. Paul and his fearless band of brothers launched out to a new continent based on a couple dead ends, a dream, and a *conclusion!* Did you catch that? "Concluding that God had called us..." It turns out Paul's heart and desire to share the gospel and plan churches was right, but his dreams were too small. While Paul sought opportunities for the Gospel locally, God opened doors for the Gospel globally! While Paul thought about the next city over, God dreamed of reaching the next continent over. Through a couple of nos and a dream, God directed Paul to Macedonia, where the first church was planted on a new continent, Europe!

As you pray and prepare and scout out a location, be happy for the NO because it's God's way of saying GO to something better.

_____ 99 _____

Be happy for the NO because it's God's
way of saying GO to something better.

_____

FLIPPING HOUSES

Although Macedonia was a new spot for Paul, it wasn't new for God. God had gone before Paul to prepare a place and the people Paul would need for the new work God was calling them to. The same was true for us and the same will be true for you.

Although God used Verlon, our mall realtor friend, to confirm our direction in moving to Clarksville, we did not have a lot of luck looking for houses with him. We gave him our budget and he lined up a mini Clarksville house tour. He tried so hard to be positive with the first house he took us to. It was across the street from a sketchy convenience store and a trailer park and was less square footage than the condo we were living in at the time in Albuquerque. As we pulled into the gravel driveway and reality hit that our budget would not let us afford much, I braced myself as we got out of the car to see the house. With paint chipping off the walls, broken windows, and an interesting aroma that was a mix of urine, secondhand smoke, and other indistinguishable odors, let's just say that house was... "unique." Verlon's faux positivity quickly turned to raw honesty as soon as we leveled with him about our feelings about the house. "Oh, what a relief," he said as we told him in no uncertain terms how offended we were at the stench of that establishment. "This place smells worse than a baby's diaper!" And with those words, we got back in our car and left as quickly as possible.

If that was all we could afford, God would have to provide miraculously for us!

As we shared our plans to move with our family and kept praying, God started lining things up. About a month before our final trip to Tennessee before the move, we found out about a house. The house was owned by an Army family in Clarksville who was the friend of a friend of our family. The husband was about to deploy and during his twelve-month deployment, his wife was moving back home with her parents. Guess where her parents lived? Albuquerque. She had a vacant house in Clarksville she wanted to rent out to a trustworthy tenant. We were trustworthy future tenants that needed a house to rent in Clarksville.

The timing could not have been better. Jenn and I met her and her dad at Starbucks in Albuquerque a couple days before our final trip to Tennessee. As we met them for the very first time, they handed us the keys to their house in Clarksville that wasn't even on the market yet. Just a week or so later as we drove into Clarksville, we walked through a house that would have been inaccessible to us had God not set us up. We didn't need a realtor to get us in that house. God opens doors no one can open.

Now that we had a place to live in Clarksville, we would need to sell our condo in Albuquerque, so we called up a friend who was a realtor. We cleaned it up, took some professional pictures, and on the market it went.

Crickets...

To say there was no foot traffic would be an understatement.

As the date of our departure drew closer, we prayed harder, cut the price deeper, and started to feel desperate. We planned an open house for a month or so before we were set to depart and even that was a flop. Almost no one came through. There was no way we could afford to rent a house in Clarksville and pay a mortgage in Albuquerque. We had to sell.

The countdown to our moving date was approaching. It went from a few weeks away to days away. We packed all our possessions into boxes and planned out a moving day. Moving day arrived and my dad and I went to pick up the rental truck and trailer while Jenn went to Einstein bagels to grab breakfast for our moving team. Standing alone in line to buy a dozen bagels, Jenn broke down crying, overwhelmed by the emotion of the moment and the stress of not being able to sell our house.

A dozen or so of our friends showed up to help us load the truck. We worked through the morning, playing a moving truck version of Tetris with our couches, chairs, bicycles, desks, and boxes.

We still hadn't sold our house, but we were filled with faith that God would send the buyer as we trusted Him.

Partway through moving day as I grabbed a box and walked it outside to the truck, my iPhone rang. It was our realtor. "Hey Sarah," I answered, wondering what kind of bad news she had for me this time. "We got an offer," she said, "but it's way less than what we are asking." She told me the amount. It wasn't what we wanted, but it still put us in the black, and more importantly, it was an answer to prayer.

"Sold! We accept the offer," I told her, very matter-of-fact. And just like that, with one arm carrying a moving box and our truck halfway packed, we sold our condo with one day left in Albuquerque before we hit the road.

Just like God had gone before Paul to provide the people and the place he would need to plant a church, 2,000 years later that same God was pulling the same moves for us. We now had a house in Clarksville and a buyer in Albuquerque.

Uprooting and moving across the nation was brand new for us, but God had been guiding and providing for His people for thousands of years already. If He could get Israel out of Egypt, He could get the Miller family out of Albuquerque. We were learning to step out and trust God even when we could barely see in front of us.

GET YOUR FEET WET

Although it took us years to determine the location and timeline, and although we've been through many challenges in the first ten years, we tell people all the time, "We are right where we are supposed to be." I want that same confidence for you. Your level of confidence is directly proportionate to your willingness to obey. There is a direct link between confidence and obedience. God-given confidence only comes when you consistently pray and believe, then let God direct your steps.

As God clarifies where and when, GO. Don't drag your feet. There will always be a list of reasons to stay where you are comfortable and connected, but if that's not where you're supposed to be, you don't want to be there. It didn't make sense for us to leave for Clarksville before we sold our condo in Albuquerque. But that was a small detail for the big God we serve. We decided to risk it all and step out anyway. God honored our faith.

99

Your level of confidence is directly
proportionate to your willingness to
obey.

God has been leading His people and honoring their faith
for years. After forty years of wandering through the wilderness,
learning a long, terrible lesson about not doubting God's ability to
keep His promises, Israel finally found themselves on the border of
Canaan, the Promised Land. They were ready. Most of them had
literally waited their entire lives for this to happen. But there was
a problem. A really big, wet problem. They couldn't just walk into
the promised land like they owned the place. The wilderness and
Canaan were divided by a natural barrier, the Jordan River. Not
only is that an issue, but it was flood season when they arrived. A
large flooding river may not seem like too big of a deal to some
young guys ready for a swim, but keep in mind there were two
million of them that needed to cross. And it wasn't two million guys
from the Israeli swim team. We are talking about entire families —
babies, kids, teenagers, moms and dads, aunts and uncles... And
if that wasn't challenging enough, they were planning on moving
into Canaan, so they were bringing all their belongings with them.

Are you starting to get the picture? The Jordan by itself would
be virtually impossible for two million people to cross, but now it was
flooding. The waters were rushing, the banks were overflowed and
treacherous. There could be hundreds of thousands of casualties
before they even entered the land! And that would be before any
battles, of which their future was full.

99

All the strategizing, planning, preparing, and team building you can do will
be great, but you're still stepping into
the unknown. Make sure you're following the God who holds it all in His
hands!

In a word, crossing into the Promised Land was *impossible*... until God gets involved.

God spoke to Joshua and laid out the plan, which involved the priests carrying the Ark of the Covenant (the visible representation of God's presence) ahead of the Jews. God told Joshua this needed to happen because "you have not passed this way before" (Joshua 3:4 ESV). I need this reminder all the time. All the strategizing, planning, preparing, and team building you can do will be great, but you're still stepping into the unknown. Make sure you're following the God who holds it all in His hands!

God was going to really test the faith of His people. God gave Joshua the plans and Joshua passed them onto the people.

"And when the soles of the feet of the priests bearing the ark of the Lord, the Lord of all the earth, shall rest in the water of the Jordan, the waters of the Jordan shall be cut off from flowing, and the waters coming down from above shall stand in one heap." (Joshua 3:13 ESV)

If the priests would trust God enough to carry their most valuable possession, the ark of the covenant, into the flooding river, God would part the river. Don't miss the weight of this moment. If they were going to see God move, the priests had to trust God and trust their leader, Joshua, enough to literally get their feet wet.

The only way you'll ever see God do the miraculous is when you are willing to step out and step in. Get your feet wet. Take God at His word. He's led you this far, He's not going to turn around and leave you now.

The only way you'll ever see God do the miraculous is when you are willing to step out and step in. Get your feet wet. Take God at His word.

You are on the edge of your Promised Land. "Consecrate yourselves, for tomorrow the Lord will do wonders among you" (Joshua 3:5 ESV).

The dream you have been chasing and the purpose you have been pursuing are here. Now is the time. Today is the day. There's no better day to trust God than today.

Be forewarned: when it's not hell itself trying to stop you, it will be high water trying to keep you on the shore where you are comfortable. Don't let anything stop you from stepping into what God has called you to. You haven't been this way before, but you are following the God who is the beginning and the end, the Alpha and the Omega, the First and the Last. He goes before you and behind you and He lives inside you. You will be uncomfortable and you will want to turn back, but if God has called you into the flooding river, step in. You will be safer in the flood with God than on the shore without Him.

99

You will be safer in the flood with God
than on the shore without Him.

One more word of warning: much of the success of your new season depends on how you finish your current season. As I quickly learned, the location is important, but so are the relationships in your life.

THREE

SMOKE SIGNALS

Be known for honor, not arson.

Pro tip: next time you are going to make a s'more, substitute the Hershey's chocolate bar for a Reese's peanut butter cup and the regular graham cracker for a chocolate graham cracker. Trust me. That tip may just be worth the price of this book. You can thank me later. "S'mores connoisseur" may be too lofty of a title to bestow upon myself, but I would gladly accept the honor.

Although I know the correct ingredients for s'mores, I once made the mistake of purchasing the wrong fuel for the fire. In a moment of laziness, I bought a Duraflame fire starter log to fuel the fire for our s'mores. My Cub Scouts troop leader would be ashamed of me.

In an act of poetic justice, my laziness backfired on me. When I arrived at the predetermined s'mores preparation location, I read the fire starter packaging. "Duraflame firelogs are not designed nor intended for use as a cooking fuel." Come to find out, the logs are to be kept out of reach of pets and small children and are toxic if consumed or ingested.

I learned an important lesson that day: the fuel for my fire is important.

It turns out that truth applies as much to our marshmallows as it does to our ministries.

The fuel behind our steps of faith is supremely important. Just like that fire starter log could simultaneously fuel a fire and be toxic, the same can be true with our motives and ministries.

Since you are reading this book, it is a pretty safe assumption that you love God and want to share the gospel in whatever context you are in, be that via planting a church, serving at a church, or in your workplace or neighborhood.

With that in mind, let's discuss how to make sure we maintain pure motives as we end one season and prepare for the next.

CHECK THE FUEL SOURCE

The prophet Jeremiah described a fire burning in his bones that he couldn't hold back (Jeremiah 20:9 ESV). As followers of Jesus, many of us have felt the same thing—a passion, a burning desire to see the lives of those around us changed by the gospel.

We want to believe our motives are pure, but let's take a moment and look beyond the flames to the fuel source.

Sometimes it's the faults or failures of others that fuel us to launch out. In the context of church planting, maybe your pastor made a promise they didn't fulfill or they wounded you in some way. If you're not careful, their faults may fuel an insatiable desire to launch out and right their wrongs in your own life or ministry.

Maybe it's not your leader's failure, maybe it's an inward fire. A burning desire to be the first, the biggest, or the best. Pioneering is a great thing, but it can be a dangerous thing when it turns from a calling to a competition.

Unmet expectations, bitterness and unforgiveness, untended wounds, and even your own prideful arrogance can also become toxic fuel sources if we are not honest and cautious. Launching out in order to prove someone wrong or prove you are the first or the best can become toxic in your life and in the lives of those around you.

I've met far too many church planters who launch out looking less like ministers and more like arsonists. It's almost like the little boys who burned stuff as kids continue that destructive behavior, but instead of burning ants with a magnifying glass, they burn bridges with attitudes and harsh words. I've noticed a tendency for zealous young men and couples to attempt to launch into a successful ministry by setting everything on fire at the church they're leaving. You know, action movie style. Douse with gasoline. Throw a match. Slo-mo walk away as everything explodes behind them. It looks epic in a movie, but will lead to epic failure in ministry.

If anybody in the Bible knew about epic fire scenes, it was Elijah. On top of Mt. Carmel (1 Kings 18 ESV), he proved God's power by calling down fire from heaven. That was a stunt that makes any Denzel Washington movie pale in comparison.

Not long after that, Elijah went to find Elisha, who God said would succeed him in ministry. As Elisha plowed a field with his oxen, Elijah walked by and "threw his cloak across his shoulders and walked away" (translation: "You're coming to my seminary. Let's go!"). Here's where the burning comes in... Without even pausing,

Elisha ran home and sacrificed his oxen on a fire made with the wooden yokes they had been wearing, making it impossible for him to go back to plowing fields. The sign was clear: he had been called into ministry and was burning his yokes so he could never go back.

Elisha burned the yokes as a step of faith, but many prospective church planters burn theirs in a rage of fury. They use the flames of their burning yokes to send smoke signals to their former leaders that they have it figured out and don't need them any longer. Then they launch out with a small band of collaterally damaged, wounded followers, and try to figure it out on their own while they medicate their wounds they won't admit exist.

The flames that should signal faith instead end up signaling fury and failure. I've been close enough to some of these leaders that I can smell the smoke from the still-smouldering fires they set.

Unfortunately, ministerial and relational arson is our default. We were born with an independent spirit. You don't have to teach an infant the words "no" or "mine;" they come very naturally. A toddler doesn't want you to do things for them, they want to prove to you they can do it on their own. Our sin nature has hardwired us to prefer independence over collaboration. If not reined in, that independent, pioneer spirit within us will naturally set off to prove a point. And instead of building relationships, we may inadvertently destroy the very ones we will need down the road. Since independence is our default setting, it takes strategy and intentionality to override it.

FINISH WELL

Finishing well was very important to me and Jenn when we left Calvary Church in Albuquerque to head to Clarksville.

Our trip to Tennessee in February 2008 was a follow-up to the dream I'd had a few months earlier at Christmas. We knew Clarksville was where we were supposed to be when the time was right, so we wanted to pray more, research further, and fulfill commitments we had already made.

When God has given you a burden for a city or a certain step of faith He is calling you to, you'll want to drop everything you're doing to get there. Resist the urge. Many years of getting it wrong has taught me that my timeline is often much different from God's.

As Jenn and I flew back home, we discussed timing. I thought my current assistant youth pastor (or as Michael Scott would say, "assistant *to the* youth pastor") would be the guy to take my role, so I was ready to begin handing things over to him. We landed back in Albuquerque on a Tuesday night, and that Wednesday, he told me he was quitting.

Interesting timing.

As God often does, He was going to use that setback as a setup for His providential timing. My assistant leaving was God telling me I wasn't leaving just yet. In that moment, I felt the Lord say, "Clarksville is the place, but now is not the time...yet. Stay faithful here until I tell you." So, Jenn and I made a few more commitments there at church, as we continued to pray for God's timing to be clear. Fast forward seven months to a mid-November Sunday morning. I was leading the youth group that morning like I had been for almost five years, when one of the staff members brought a guy named AJ over to meet me. He was looking for a place to get involved serving. He was thinking of serving with middle or high school, and our volunteer coordinator pointed him to middle school. I had never experienced what I was about to experience with AJ, nor have I since. As I shook his hand for the very first time and learned his name, I had this very distinct feeling that I was shaking the hand of the guy who would replace me. Normally, that would feel threatening, but this time it was exciting. We had been praying for months for the right person to come along, and as crazy as it seemed, I was pretty sure this was the guy. I took him to my office, showed him around, introduced him to the students and leaders, and kept quietly praying over the following days, weeks, and months.

It was the following week that I decided it was time to tell my boss what God had been stirring in our hearts. I remember nervously setting up the meeting with his assistant, then walking into his office on the day of the meeting.

As I shared the news of my coming departure and our potential timeline, he asked the question I had anticipated. "So who's going to take your spot?" he asked.

I didn't know how he would receive the answer even I thought was crazy, but this was my chance. "Well," I paused, nervously laughing as I led into the answer, "You're probably going to think I'm crazy, but I'll go ahead and say it anyway... I think I just met him on Sunday. His name is AJ, and I have this odd feeling he's the guy."

"We'll see about that," he replied.

Yes we would see about that.

Before we move forward, while we're on the topic of meeting with your superior, let me encourage you to move forward with that meeting. You may be tempted to just leave, or turn in a two weeks' notice, or send them a text message letting them know last Sunday was your last Sunday. Stop it. You shouldn't end a dating relationship that way and you certainly shouldn't end a ministry partnership that way.

I understand the intimidation factor. Originally, my boss told me not to tell our pastor right away. He advised me to wait at least into the beginning of the next year, just in case my pastor's response was, "Well if you're going to leave eventually, there's the door." Thankfully he responded in the opposite way, and *sent* us out months later instead of *kicking* us out.

99

How they respond is up to them, and how you respond to what God is telling you to do is up to you.

Don't let the intimidation or fear of their potential reaction drive you. Those aren't what matter and there's nothing you can do about them anyway. How they respond is up to them and how you respond is up to you. You can only control one of them, so don't let the other bother you. You just do your part. Don't leave a minute earlier or a minute later than God tells you to leave. And if you share your dream and are shown the door, don't panic. You may not have seen that coming, but God did. Trust Him, even when the timeline is different than what you had in mind.

TIMING IS EVERYTHING

Chances are, you'll be ready to leave sooner than you should leave. I was. Most church planters and big-risk faith walkers I've met were born with a God-given entrepreneurial pioneer spirit. We like to start things. And when you get the vision of the future in your mind, it will begin to dominate your thoughts. You'll feel like a sprinter in the starting blocks or a bottle rocket with the fuse lit. You'll want to name it, plan it, build it, and as you shift your focus toward the future, your focus will naturally shift off of the present.

I'm not proud to admit it, but I was tempted to launch out much sooner than I did simply because of my competitive nature. I wanted to hit the ground running before some of the other people around me did. If you're looking for a great way to fail at church planting or the unique calling on your life, there's a good one. Turn it into a competition and try to do it bigger, better, and faster than other people. I still have plenty to learn about God's timing, but one of the big things I've learned is that my timeline is not only different from God's, but it is also different from other people's. Just as the people I'm reaching are different, so is the timeline in which I'm reaching them. The measure of success is not who launched it or built it faster. The measure of success is how closely we walked with Jesus and how obediently we lived. Remember that independent arsonist nature we discussed earlier? You don't just beat it once, you'll have to keep harnessing it and reining it in throughout your life and ministry.

The measure of success is not who launched it or built it faster. The measure of success is how closely we walked with Jesus and how obediently we lived.

DISTRACTIONS AND EXCUSES

Once Jenn and I made up our minds and put the wheels into motion, distractions and excuses started coming in waves. One day I got an email from a pastor in Albuquerque who wanted to meet up to talk ministry. He told me they were reworking their youth group and he wanted to talk about some of the things that were working for us. I arrived at Starbucks, got my sugary latte drink (I had yet to learn the ways of black coffee), and sat down to talk youth ministry. That's when he blindsided me. "Let me cut to the chase," he said. "I'm not here to talk youth ministry as much as I am to talk about you coming to work for our church. After all, Calvary doesn't pay you that well, right?" I sat there speechless, shocked at what I was hearing. He went on… "We want to hire you to be our rock star (his literal words). You can come in and do whatever you want and tell us how you want it, and we'll do it." Our conversation didn't last much longer as I politely shut him down, grabbed my still-hot coffee, and walked out. I couldn't believe they were trying to hire a rock star instead of a pastor, which are on opposite ends of the ministry spectrum. What was this, *American Idol?*

A quick word about assembling a team: if your hiring or recruiting strategy is reminiscent of *America's Got Talent*, solely focusing on getting people who will increase ratings and revenue, watch out. You'll end up hiring a prima donna diva who will make demands, want the spotlight, and either burn out, burn others out, or morally fail out of ministry quickly. A hiring strategy like that is a recipe for disaster, and you're a fool for approaching it that way. Ministry is not a stage for rock stars; it's a platform for the gospel, which is all about serving others and humbling ourselves. Paul said to "have this mind in you that was also in Christ Jesus…" (Philippians 2 ESV). Remember that? Jesus told His bickering, murmuring, constantly competing disciples, "…those who are regarded as rulers of the Gentiles lord it over them, and their high officials exercise authority over them. *Not so with you…*" (Mark 10:42-43 NIV). Christian leaders don't lead like other leaders. We don't do what we do to make a name for ourselves. We're here to point to the One whose name is above every name.

I went back to church that day and reported back to my overseeing pastor. To my surprise, the guy I had met with used to work at the church years prior! It wasn't long before he received a phone call and an earful from my boss. Apparently word made it back to our senior pastor and he decided to reward my loyalty with a bonus and a raise! That was an unexpected perk for my decision to dismiss the coffee-luring talent scout from the church across the city. Interestingly, not only did the pay raise encourage me, it also temporarily distracted me. I mistakenly thought I owed my pastor some more time since he was paying me more.

In the coming weeks and months, if it wasn't an opportunity for a new position or a pay raise that gave me an excuse not to move, it was fear of the unknown, watching others try and fail, thinking about how good we had it, not wanting to leave my mom by herself in Albuquerque, and about a hundred other things.

But we had to do it. We couldn't keep giving into the excuses. There would always be reasons not to leave.

The clincher finally came when I knew it was time to tell my pastor about our plans. Those same nerves were back as I set up the meeting with his assistant and counted down the days until I would make our move official. Thankfully, the meeting couldn't have gone much better. He was so encouraging, accommodating, and excited for us. He was excited for the step of faith we were about to take and even told me he'd send me out with a couple months' extra pay to help us as we got our feet on the ground.

I had no idea that leaving well would turn out to be one of the most strategic, helpful, life-giving decisions we would make as we prepared for launch.

GOD WILL NOT HONOR DISHONOR

I admit, in many ways, the circumstances surrounding us leaving and launching out were ideal. We had great, Godly, gracious leaders who were supportive and excited for us. I hope the same is true for you. And one day, when the roles are reversed, I hope you'll be the same way: supportive, excited, and encouraging.

Not everyone will be able to leave under such favorable circumstances though. So does a dishonorable leader justify a dishonorable exit? I guess maybe you should consult the former shepherd boy turned giant-slayer and up-and-coming king of Israel, David, for an answer to that question. He spent years of his life while under God's anointing, running for his life from King Saul, whom he was unwilling to harm. He had some very clear opportunities and, many would argue, the justification to kill King Saul or at least to stop the threats to his life. At one point, David had King Saul cornered in a cave, sneaked up behind him and with a dagger in hand, when most would have taken the opportunity to cut his jugular, David settled for slightly vandalizing a small corner of Saul's robe. And then he felt bad about it! David knew that God honors honor and will not tolerate dishonor.

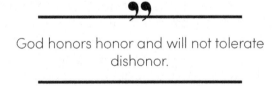

God honors honor and will not tolerate dishonor.

You could also ask a whole host of people in Moses' day

about God's thoughts on dishonoring His leaders. Moses was an imperfect leader. God had to take him through so much pre-ministry training that he didn't even get his start in ministry till he was eighty years old...after he had murdered a guy and got sent to the wilderness to take care of a bunch of dirty sheep for forty years. Talk about a rough start! Most people graduate from seminary in their twenties or thirties. Moses was about five decades behind. Years later, when Moses' brother and sister, Aaron and Miriam, decided they had had enough of getting bossed around by their older brother, they stood up to him. God wouldn't have it. He struck Miriam's hands with leprosy, turning them into a graphic visual of how disgusting dishonor is to the Lord. Only a couple chapters later, a guy named Korah, who apparently had to learn firsthand instead of by example, led more than 250 men in an uprising against Moses and Aaron. Do you think God was ok with that? The Bible says, "The earth opened its mouth and swallowed them up, with their households and all the people who belonged to Korah and all their goods. So they and all that belonged to them went down alive into Sheol, and the earth closed over them, and they perished from the midst of the assembly" (Numbers 16:32-33 ESV). The earth ate them for lunch! If that wasn't ridiculous enough, God still wasn't done. Korah had 250 rebels that had risen up with him. The story goes on to say that, "fire came out from the Lord and consumed the 250 men offering the incense" (Numbers 16:35 ESV). Speaking of epic fire scenes, there's one for the books!

In summary, here are God's thoughts on dishonoring your leaders: leprosy, man-swallowing-earthquakes, and lightning strikes.

Do I really think God is going to zap you with a skin disease or a bolt of lightning for dishonoring your leader or ending your current season in a less than favorable way? No, but the precedent is set. And for those of you who think these David or Moses examples are outdated, the principle is all across the New Testament too. Try Romans 13 on for size.

> **"Let every person be subject to the governing authorities. For there is no authority except from God, and those that exist have been instituted by God. Therefore whoever resists the authorities resists what God has appointed, and those who resist will incur judgment."**
> **(Romans 13:1-2 ESV)**

---

*If God can't trust you to be under, He
can't trust you to be over.*

I can already hear the outcry. "But you don't understand! You don't know what my pastor did." You're right. I don't. But I do know you are not the agent of God's vengeance on your pastor or leader. Let God deal with them. Honor your leaders and leave respectably. Even if you disagree with your pastor or the leader that is over you, and *even if they're in sin,* God put them in that position. He didn't cause their sin and He's not okay with it, but as God, He is aware of it. I'm not advocating condoning sin; I'm saying that even when you're leaving under less than ideal circumstances, you can (and should) leave honorably. It's easy to justify burning your bridges when you feel mistreated, underappreciated, and/or overworked, but even then, you can finish well. Honor the leaders God has set in place. Don't bad-mouth them. Don't gossip. Don't sow division. That's not the foundation you want to build a ministry on. How do you expect God to honor your new position of leadership when you won't honor the leadership He's already put in place over you? In other words, if God can't trust you to be under, He can't trust you to be over.

If you're brazen enough to bowl over and publicly disrespect someone in authority over you, what prevents you from doing that with someone under you, say at the church you plan on starting? Peter addresses this when he says, "Care for the flock that God has entrusted to you. Watch over it willingly, not grudgingly—not for what you will get out of it, but because you are eager to serve God. Don't lord it over the people assigned to your care, but lead them by your own good example" (1 Peter 5:2-3 NLT).

If you get in the habit of pushing people out of the way when they interfere with your plans or threaten your territory, you'll never survive as a shepherd. In fact, you'd better hit the gym because Peter goes on to say that "God opposes the proud" (1 Peter 5:5 ESV). Pride squares you off against God Himself. Spoiler alert: that's a fight you'll never win.

YOUR FUTURE IS NEEDY

I wasn't always a crier, but church planting has changed that. I cry more now than I have in a long time. Blame the kids. Blame the stress. Blame what you want, but I think ministry tends to have a heart-softening effect the more you're around hurting people. Be forewarned though: if you let it, ministry can have the opposite effect if you're not careful. You can end up with a calloused, uncaring heart if you don't learn to love and forgive.

Before moving to Clarksville, I'm pretty sure I had never cried on the phone to another grown man before. But it's happened a few times since we started the church. Whether I'm choking back tears or just giving into sobbing, I've only ever cried on the phone with a pastor or leader I once served with. I never expected that part of ministry...then again, there are plenty of unexpected experiences coming your way that others who have gone before you have already traversed. You'll need their comfort and guidance.

I heard someone say once, "Your resources are in your relationships." If anything about my life and ministry is true, this is it. None of us will reach our full potential or get to where God has called us on our own. We need each other. We are better together.

None of us will reach our full potential
or get to where God has called us on
our own. We need each other. We are
better together.

I've spent more time in conversation with my pastor in the last three years of ministry than I did in the three I spent working with him...and we live 1,200 miles apart now! He's had me out to guest speak, taken our family out to dinner when we are in town, made a couple trips to Clarksville to speak for me, visited used bookstores with me, and even spent a couple months giving me weekly sermon feedback! He even took a Polaroid with me, posing yearbook-style on my kitchen table. If you ever come over to my house, I'll show you the picture. Leadership is lonely enough. I can't imagine how much harder this experience would be had I burned my bridges and ruined the relationships I had. Unfortunately, I know plenty of people who have done that.

They're floating around as the center of their little ministry solar system trying to reinvent wheels that were invented long ago. Unfortunately, the temper tantrum they threw or their attempt at displaying their superior knowledge has cut off the access they could have had to much needed resources and wisdom. Here's the hard reality: whether you want to admit it or not, your pastor and the leaders over you have more experience and knowledge than you do. Tap into that wealth of knowledge. You'll need someone to ask questions of, seek advice from, and probably cry to (even if you think you're not a crier!).

TRAIN YOUR REPLACEMENT NOW

Speaking of leaving, Denver, one of my friends who moved from Albuquerque to Clarksville with us, left Clarksville and moved back to Albuquerque around the one-year mark. We had just finished rebuilding after the flood and were preparing to reopen within the next few weeks when he left. I still remember when he told me he was leaving. I was sitting in my office chair in my upstairs office next to the pool table our landlord had left behind. I couldn't believe what I was hearing. In his defense, he had warned me. He had never promised to be with us forever, but he had committed to being there for the first year. He plowed with us for the hardest year, then left before he got to see the fruit of our labor as we relaunched after the flood. As painful as it was when he decided to leave, he did it the best that he could have. He gave me plenty of notice, had prayerfully considered his decision, and served and worked hard up until the day he and his gold Toyota Tacoma rolled out of Clarksville.

Unfortunately, not everyone has left so gracefully over the years. Speaking from the Lead Pastor perspective, there's nothing more frustrating than someone in a key position getting an idea to leave, then vanishing. It's happened a time or two over the years and it always leaves confusion, questions, and chaos in its wake. I've had some rough jobs over the years, but I even left my first job at Great American Car Wash with more dignity and respect than that! Don't you think you owe it to those you've been leading, pastoring, and ministering with to not leave them hanging in your absence?

Even Jesus' sudden departure wasn't really sudden. He departed after three years of miracles, promises, on-the-job ministry training with the disciples, and many, many warnings and reminders of His plans. He could not have been more clear about His plans. Similar to my shock about Denver's departure, the disciples were only caught off guard because of their own ignorance.

The preparation and launch period is so challenging because you may find your heart in two places. If you're like us, we loved serving where we were, but we knew our time was coming to a close and we were so excited to launch out. As antsy as we felt, we knew that part of leaving well was honoring our leaders and the team, students, and staff we'd be leaving behind.

Sometimes people choose not to train or delegate to others because they think this ensures job security. As though if they're the only ones who can do the job, their boss will always have to keep them around. If you worked for me, you would learn that nothing could be further from the truth. Part of our hiring process is constantly reminding ourselves that we don't hire doers; we hire leaders. Sure, leaders need to be doers and get the job done, but more importantly, they should be constantly bringing others alongside them, training others for the work of the ministry (see Ephesians 4). I tell our staff that as long as they are working themselves out of a job, they'll always have a job. You'll never train too many people at Awaken Church. In fact, the more people you train and the more ministry you give away, the more we will work hard to ensure you have a job at Awaken. Why do I bring this up? Because no matter which stage you are in with ministry, it's the right time to train others up. As you keep your head down, heart open to the Lord, and your hands hard at work training others in the work of the ministry, when God tells you it's time to go, your replacement will already be trained up and ready to go! You won't have to worry about leaving someone hanging because you'll be surrounded by a team of leaders that will take the ministry you've been leading even further than you could on your own.

Finishing well does not happen by accident. It requires time, strategy, and intentionality. Before the checkered flag falls on your current season and the green flag ushers you into the next, make sure you've done all you can to finish with integrity.

As long as you're following Jesus, there are plenty of fires ahead. Start your new ministry season marked with honor, not with arson. Leave with honor and watch God honor your hard work.

Finish well.

—————— **99** ——————

Start your new ministry season marked with honor, not with arson. Leave with honor and watch God honor your hard work.

PART TWO

BOOTS ON THE GROUND

FOUR
BROOMS, BUSES, AND LUNCH BREAKS

Do what you have to so you can do what you're called to.

"Where am I?" panicked, I frantically thought to myself as I woke up realizing I had no idea where I was.

"What time is it?"

"What day is it?"

"Wait… Is this the women's dressing room?"

It was 3:00am on a Tuesday morning. I was in the women's dressing room at a shopping mall on the Army Post. This scene would be unsettling for anyone, but especially for a guy...in the women's dressing room. This wasn't a case of public intoxication like it may sound; it was a case of on-the-job exhaustion. Before I get to that story, let me back up...

UNLOAD/RELOAD

My final day on staff at our church in Albuquerque had come and gone. Our moving truck was loaded and our hearts were already in Tennessee, even though our bodies had not yet arrived. I did a wedding for two of our friends on Sunday night then we rolled out of Albuquerque on Monday morning with my final bacon and green chile breakfast burrito in hand.

As we rumbled out of town, Jenn and our two-year old daughter, Emery, stayed one final night with some friends before they flew out to meet us in our new Tennessee home. In a freak accident, Jenn fumbled a marble table top, dropping it directly on her toe. Although we lack the x-rays to prove it, we are convinced it broke her toe. She called me in tears to explain what happened. My six-month pregnant wife hobbling through airports with our daughter, stroller, car seat, and bags promised to be challenging enough. Now with a broken toe? Please, no. We prayed and the only explanation is that God healed her toe that night. She trekked those airports the next day like a champ without even a limp!

Meanwhile on I-40 East, my dad and I had more than 1,200 miles to travel across five states. Our Budget rental truck pulling a trailer with my truck on top was unable to get above sixty miles per hour. About seventy miles past Oklahoma City, all the dashboard lights came on and we quickly pulled over to the side of the road as steam enveloped the hood. We made a phone call then passed the time as we waited. Three hours later, after sweating, chasing fireflies in the dark, and scratching our fresh mosquito bites, a tow truck pulled up. We offloaded my truck and followed the Budget truck as it was towed back into Oklahoma City, where we took an unexpected pit stop for the night.

The next morning, they informed us our truck could not be fixed and all of our stuff would have to be unloaded and reloaded into a new truck, promising a moving crew was on the way. My dad and I, wanting to expedite the process, began unloading the truck that took ten adults half a day to load. Temperatures kept climbing along with the humidity. I could be wrong, but I'm pretty sure the asphalt on that 100° Oklahoma City summer day was close to the temperature of the surface of the sun.

The aforementioned moving crew finally arrived after we had completely unloaded the truck and partially reloaded a new truck. Great timing, guys! By the end of the day, we had cleaned out a nearby vending machine of all of their $1.50 water bottles and heat stroke was setting in. We gladly let the moving crew finish as we collapsed, shirts off, in the dry and weary wasteland that was the Oklahoma City parking lot.

Looking around the parking lot of the repair shop, our already negative opinion of Budget rental trucks diminished even further as we counted more than a dozen other Budget trucks also awaiting repair. Was this a Budget rental truck graveyard?

Once the truck was reloaded, we finally departed, saying good riddance to Oklahoma City with our Chick-Fil-A sandwiches in hand. We drove into the night, stopped at a cheap hotel for the night, then finally rolled into Clarksville the following afternoon, exhausted and exhilarated.

As me, my dad, and my six-months pregnant wife unloaded the moving truck for the second time, the sun set on our first official night in Clarksville, the stifling humidity reminded us we were no longer in the desert. Our new neighbors peeked out at us through their blinds, wondering who the new neighbors were. As if getting there wasn't hard enough, now the real work began.

APPLY, FISH, NAP, REPEAT

I was unemployed when we arrived in Clarksville. Unemployment sounded too corporate and vanilla, so the guys and I preferred the term "funemployment" during this rare season where we would go fishing and take naps in between bouts of job applications. Jenn and I had a rental house, a car, a baby on the way, and lots of vision and faith, but no income beside a couple months' worth of pay from our church in Albuquerque. I applied for virtually every job available, and even some jobs that weren't available. Lowe's, Home Depot, Sam's Club, Staples... You name it, and I probably applied for it. To no avail. When I heard about a local janitorial company hiring for the midnight shift, I was interested. "How hard can it be to clean stuff?" I thought. After all of the promising places I had applied, Dust Busters Plus was my first Clarksville employer.

My first midnight janitorial shift was at a local nursing home, stripping and waxing the floors while the tenants stared blankly at us for hours. "Hey Wanda, shouldn't you be in bed or playing Bridge or something right now? And stop that incessant rocking. You're creeping me out."

After the nursing home job, Dust Busters won the bid to clean the mall on the nearby Army Post. "*Won* the bid" sounds exciting, but don't get too excited. It was great for the company, but that meant I "won" the opportunity to sweep, vacuum, strip and wax floors, clean windows, and scrub public toilets, Monday through Friday, midnight to 8:00 am! The job was about as glamorous as it sounds.

I have a lot of stories from the couple months I worked there, including the women's dressing room story. Although the details are a bit hazy, apparently, after sweeping and vacuuming the women's clothing department for a few hours, I decided I had earned a break. I don't recall sitting down or falling asleep, and I have no idea how much time passed. It may have been ten minutes or a couple hours. Sheer exhaustion created some kind of partial amnesia that the ensuing panic cleared up. Ever been there? It's one thing to wake up disoriented in your own bed, but entirely another to find yourself in a mystery dressing room — and a women's dressing room at that!

The only "plus" of working at Dust Busters Plus was the reliable paycheck and minimal overtime. The hours were grueling, the work was boring, and my mind was wandering. I didn't want "making money" to be my focus, but I obviously had to make money somehow. I tried to keep an upbeat attitude about the job, but the 11:30 pm drive in to work each night was often depressing. I remember calling a mentor-friend of mine once at 10:30 pm. I didn't expect to cry, but the tears just started flowing. Before I knew it, I was a grown man, sobbing and slobbering on the phone to another grown man, wondering why I was here and if all of this was a crazy mistake. I knew it wasn't, but part of me wished it was. Giving up and moving back to Albuquerque felt like our equivalent of Israel wanting to go back to Egypt. I knew Albuquerque was not where I was supposed to be, and I knew I was in the land God had promised us, but the comfort of Egypt sure sounded nice every once in a while.

Once I psyched myself up each night, I would head inside, grab a broom, a dustpan, and some cleaning supplies, and get to work. Thankfully, some great preachers like Steven Furtick, Judah Smith, and Matt Chandler swept and vacuumed floors with me via podcasts for hours on end each night.

WEARING A LOT OF HATS

One of the more humbling moments in our first few months came when I entered a photo contest for a local coffee shop, Lasaters Coffee. Typically, I'm not one to enter a photo contest, but when you're strapped and the grand prize is $250 cash, you pay attention. I read the rules, then grabbed my digital camera and went to work. Unfortunately I didn't win the grand prize, but I did win first place. My prize was…wait for it… "Not cash." Normally, I would have been happy to win anything at all, but I was pretty sure that a jacket emblazoned with the Lasaters Coffee logo wasn't going to pay any bills. I had jackets; it was cash I didn't have much of. As I went to claim my prize, I walked into the Lasaters Coffee headquarters and introduced myself to the founder and owner, Mat. We small talked for a moment, then he congratulated me on winning and asked my jacket size. I swallowed my pride and started into my humbling request. "About the prize…" I said, preparing to eat some humble pie, "Would it be possible, instead of the jacket, for you to give me the money you were going to spend on the jacket? Our family could really use the cash." He was so gracious and handed me a crisp $100 bill! He didn't have to order a jacket and I was $100 richer (less poor?). Win-win!

Meanwhile, the midnight janitor shift wasn't getting any easier. Just trying to adjust my body to the midnight shift was hard enough, but add in the emotional toll it quickly took on my marriage and family, and I knew it wouldn't work for long. Jenn would be heading to bed as I was getting ready to head into work. I can still remember a few nights where she cried as I hugged her. I'd get home in the morning and go to bed as she and our daughter, Emery, got up and going for the day. I scanned every job option I could find, and finally an ad caught my eye: "Hiring Part Time School Bus Drivers! Pay starts at $12.30/hr!" "School bus driver?!" I thought to myself. "I can handle that." After all, I was a former Youth Pastor. I knew how to handle kids. And thanks to a job at an auction house years prior where I drove tow trucks and forklifts, I knew all about driving big vehicles. So I applied, and within a couple weeks, I was attending training classes and learning to drive a school bus. I parallel parked a seventy-foot-long school bus, executed some flawless K-turns, wove that giant yellow taxi in and out of cones forward and backward, and learned to do a full bus check, bumper to bumper. Not long after I started training, I passed my CDL test, and I was in! What's up, Clarksville Montgomery County School System? You have a new bus driver in town. Literally. Navigating the seemingly unplanned, winding, abruptly-ending, multiple-named Clarksville streets without GPS and with an outdated route sheet is a story for a different book, but it was an adventure, that's for sure. I happily turned in my two weeks' notice at Dust Busters Plus, and traded my squeegee for a steering wheel.

For the first few months, my only job was driving a bus. I'd leave for the bus yard around 5:30 am, get my route assignment for the day, head out to pick kids up for school, then head to the library for a few hours and lock myself in one of their stale, nothing-on-the-walls, windowed study rooms. I'd study for a few hours for the next message I'd be preaching at our months-old church, then head back to the bus lot to get a bus and pick kids up from school. It was this stage in pastoring and preaching that I learned the importance of taking my study notes with me so I could study anywhere I got a chance. The library wasn't the only place I studied; I studied on a school bus awaiting dispatch, in the breakroom when I wasn't assigned a bus, in the hospital cafeteria with a Red Bull and a chicken sandwich hours after our second daughter was born, and in a majority of Clarksville's coffee shops. Winter was rough that year, and I ended up not driving nearly as much I needed to, so I had to get an additional job. That's where my first place photo contest win came in handy. I went back to the warehouse where I had met Mat Lasater, and he hired me part time to help with social media, the website, and shipping and receiving.

Church Planter? Check.

School bus driver and wrangler of nefarious middle school students? Check.

Warehouse and website manager? Check.

Exhausted? Check. What is sleep?

I had never worked so hard at so many simultaneous jobs and made so little money.

As if I wasn't busy enough, and since I still wasn't making enough money to pay our bills, I also decided to start up some freelance graphic design. It didn't take long for that to take off, and before I knew it, a normal day consisted of getting to the bus yard at 5:30 am, picking kids up and dropping them off at school, studying at the library, heading to the coffee warehouse for a French press (or three) and five hours of work, then home to slam down some dinner, say hey to the family, and do some design work until midnight or I collapsed, whichever came first.

The freelance design work started to take off, and eventually led to a job as an album designer with InPop Records, a Christian record label in Nashville. I primarily worked from home, but drove into their office in Brentwood, about an hour and fifteen minutes from my house, once per week. I went to photo shoots with bands, designed CD covers and layouts (remember CDs, anyone?), and got to meet some really cool people. If you ever pick up the Newsboys album, *God's Not Dead*, check the inside cover for my name! For many graphic designers, this was a dream job.

All this time, on top of the three or four jobs I was working, I was also working hard to build Awaken Church. I was teaching twice weekly, working multiple jobs, trying to make sure my family was taken care of. For our very first Good Friday service in April 2010, my boss wouldn't let me take the day off for our mid-day Good Friday service. So, I strategically took my lunch break with enough time to grab my notes, change clothes, and get to the church. I pulled into the parking lot, straightened my tie, greeted a couple dozen people who had gathered for the service, taught a message, took communion, then got back in my truck to head back to work before my lunch break was over.

With all of the jobs I was working and money I was making, none of it was enough, in multiple ways. Not only were these jobs not enough to fully pay our bills, but they weren't enough to make me satisfied. The job many designers would have called their "dream job" was just a way to pay bills for me. It's not that I didn't enjoy it, it's just that it wasn't what I was created to do and it's not why I lived in Tennessee. I knew there was something different that God had called me to.

LEARN TO LOVE WHAT YOU HATE

Paychecks are a necessary evil. We have to have them, and sometimes we have to work a job (or two or three) we don't love so we can do the work we love and are called to. At the onset, your calling won't fund itself.

Ideally, as you launch out to plant a church or step out in faith in some way, there will be enough money in the budget for you to receive full time pay from the beginning. With the right strategy and funding, it can happen, and with church planting organizations like ARC (Association of Related Churches), funding is becoming more of a possibility these days. Full time pay from the beginning is not my story though. I wasn't hired full time at the church till about two years in.

I know "hate" is a strong word, but it's pretty accurate when it comes to my time mopping floors at the PX. There were some good times and some not-so-terrible times, but over all, I didn't love it. I tried to make the best of it though.

You should see the look of shock and disdain when I tell people I used to be a school bus driver. By the sound of their reactions, it seems most people would rather unclog toilets than manage students and navigate streets. "That must have been quite the job!" they say about bus driving. Yes it was. I didn't love the hours or the pay or the freezing cold buses in the dark at 5:30 am in January, but I made the best of it.

The coffee warehouse job was one of the better jobs. That coupled with bus driving and graphic design made for long days, but again, I made the best of it. I was also thankful for the high caffeine content that position came with!

My favorite job was graphic design. I love the creative

process and making things look great on screen and in print. I was doing things I loved and had thought about going to college for.

Love it or hate it, none of it was why I had moved to Clarksville. That made all of it somewhat frustrating. I knew we were in a season and it wouldn't always be that way. I knew God would give me the strength to take care of my family and lead the church at the capacity I could handle.

By God's grace, I'm still alive, married, my kids love me, and the church is growing.

99

Being faithful and working hard at your job is also a calling. Crush it at work just like you'd crush it if Jesus was right there. Because He is.

By the way, planting a church, taking steps of faith, and loving your family are not your only callings. Being faithful and working hard at your job is also a calling. Crush it at work just like you'd crush it if Jesus was right there. Because He is.

RETROFIT

Finding Clarksville was quite the journey already, but finding where to hold our Bible study and church services was another journey altogether.

The first place I taught the Bible in Clarksville was in a living room. One of the first couples we met in Clarksville opened their home to us and encouraged us to start a midweek Bible study as we built a small gathering and prepared for launch. From the start, we wanted to build a church that was open and welcoming to everyone. Maybe I should have specified that I was referring to our species, the human race. In addition to a few families gathering in that living room, the couple also let their dogs roam free throughout the Bible studies. My years as a middle school youth pastor trained me in the fine art of teaching through distractions, but having a seventy-pound golden retriever lick my hand and whine for me to pet him while I'm expositing Romans 12 pushed the boundaries of my experience! We made it work though.

After a couple months' search for a non-living-room venue, I was excited to finally find a potential place near a busy crossroads in the middle of the city. It used to be a tanning salon called Tropical Tanz and was complete with small tanning rooms divided by faux-wooden walls and extra-large electrical outlets to handle the voltage of tanning beds in each makeshift room. Unfortunately they took the tanning beds when they moved out. Teaching, tithing, and tanning sounds like a great combo to me, but maybe that's for someone else to explore.

The whole space was only 1,000 square feet, but it fit our budget, so we went for it. We signed a lease and spent one Friday night with a small group of our new friends getting the space church-ready. Upon contacting Buildings and Codes (which, it turns out you should do prior to signing a lease and renovating), we found out the old Tropical Tanz was zoned for retail, not assembly, meaning we could only have fifteen people inside at once. We had more than fifteen kids already, not to mention the adults, so this immediately posed a problem.

Our landlord graciously let us out of the lease penalty-free, but now we had a few new problems. We had already printed flyers with our address and were promoting a launch date that was only about three weeks away. Now we didn't have a building, and from what we had learned about this new thing called "humidity," we knew meeting outside would rarely be an option. The next day after we backed out of our lease, I frantically drove the city, calling every number I could find on any "for lease" sign I saw. We met landlords at an old cell phone store, a tiny auxiliary building outside a Methodist Church, and I called about everything from a former hair salon to storefronts to a Seventh-Day Adventist church who conveniently meet on Saturdays instead of Sundays.

Nothing came of any of those until I made the sad, dejected drive home. I made one final call about a place I saw, just to get turned down again. But it turned out that the landlord had another property down on Riverside that sounded like something that might work for us. The team and I met him there the next day and signed a six-month lease on the hood of my maroon 2004 Toyota Highlander. The space was a 2,400 square-foot cubicle-filled former office space that a family of spiders had now turned into their workspace. If you could look past the cobwebs and cubicles, you could envision a future worship space on one side and kids classrooms on the other. It would need a lot of TLC, but we were ready.

I signed the lease on September 8 and our launch date was eleven days later on September 19. We spent every night for the following week and a half until about midnight or later pulling down years-old cracked navy blue wallpaper, sanding glue off the walls while wearing masks, tearing out cubicles, installing chair rails, painting, decorating, and showing the spiders what we thought of their presence in our space. Not only did we prefer to worship without dogs, but we are even more so a spider-free church. Sorry, Charlotte. A week and a half later, the space was ready for opening night.

In addition to renovating a tanning salon, old office spaces, and a workout space, we've done a lot more over the last few years. We celebrated the church's fifth birthday by purchasing the entire shopping center where we had been renting a few storefronts. I walked into the bank as a tenant and walked out as an owner, carrying a pocketful of keys. Since we bought the shopping center, we've converted a former loan company's space into a cafe and collaborative workspace as well as a former tattoo studio into a green room and video studio.

OUT WITH THE STAINED GLASS

All of our buildings and meeting spaces make sense in light of a dream that took place before we moved to Clarksville. Nate, a good friend, church planting sidekick, and now Executive Pastor of Awaken Church, dreamed about the work God was calling us to. In the dream, he and I and our wives walked into an old, abandoned church building complete with stained glass windows and pews. In the dream, we went straight to work getting the building ready to use. Whereas many people may have polished up the windows and refinished the pews, we began removing them. We took down the steeple, removed the stained glass, and substituted modern chairs for the pews.

Since then, we have often wondered if God would lead us to an abandoned church building. Although that dream has not been fulfilled literally so far, we have seen it fulfilled figuratively as we work to dismantle and refresh the old strains and chains of tradition and religion. We may not physically remove the stained glass, but in a way, that's what we've done by reaching unchurched people in very non-traditional ways.

We are not anti-tradition by any means. We're just wired

differently. I don't wear slacks and I'm rarely in a tie, except for a funeral or a wedding. People have regularly told me I don't look like a pastor and I wear that designation proudly. I've been told my tattoos and the casual, non-traditional atmosphere of our church makes unchurched people feel comfortable. I met a tattoo artist at our church recently who came because she met me when I had gone in for a tattoo. She figured if the pastor had tattoos, maybe her tattoos, pink hair, and bull ring would be welcome. And she was right. We love stories like that. We are thankful for the traditional, liturgical churches that reach people who lean that direction, but they are not us and we are not them. That's a good thing! Lots of different churches reach lots of different people.

Throughout the life of our church, we've taken old things and made them fresh and relevant. It's become a passion of ours. We love to see something that looks old and unusable, envision something fresh, then transform it.

So much of our journey of following Jesus has been about making the best of what we have. Circumstances, resources, and timing are often less than ideal, but whether it was coming up with creative ways to pay our bills or creatively transforming buildings, we want to creatively and faithfully use what is in our hands.

DANG, THAT GOSPEL LOOKS GOOOOD!

A guy at our church runs a handyman business as his main source of income, but also relies heavily on his side hustle, fireworks stands. He manages a few dozen around the Clarksville and southern Kentucky area and if you talk to him any time within a four-month radius of July 4 or New Years Eve, he's probably in the middle of hauling a truckload of fireworks somewhere. He's provided our family and church with hours of explosive fun over the years. In fact, my kids still talk about a multiple-round mortar called "To Hell and Back" he gave us once. In New Mexico, we could barely legally light sparklers. Tennessee is the home of the free and the brave, and the sky is the limit. Literally.

You could call Dennis a tentmaker, and not just because he runs fireworks tents. The term "tentmaker" comes from the mention of Paul's side hustle in Acts 18. The term carries different meanings and roles in our day since I don't know a single person who actually makes tents as their job, besides Dennis, I guess. But Paul literally made tents and worked with leather for a living so he didn't have to take a salary from the church (although he mentions in 2 Corinthians 8 that he had every right to be on the payroll). The term "tentmaker" has come to refer to bivocational ministry. Whether you drive buses, design logos, dress mannequins, or deliver mail, if you're working outside the church on top of ministry to pay your bills, you're a tentmaker. Thankfully you're in good company.

Moses was a shepherd/speaker.

Jesus was a carpenter/healer/revolutionary.

Luke was a doctor/historian/missionary.

Paul was a tentmaker/church planter.

My friend Ryan runs a handyman business and serves in multiple areas around our church.

My friend Carlos does ministry by serving at his church and co-running a clothing brand called Biblical Merch with his wife, Ashley. They use the proceeds from the clothing sales to reach into the homeless and hopeless on Skid Row in L.A. It doesn't yet pay the bills yet for them, so Carlos has been working hard for years as an Army recruiter.

Before we could hire our Kids Ministry Director, Mindy, full-time, she worked at a local pottery painting studio, called Horsefeathers, to help make ends meet at home.

On top of his job as a youth pastor, my friend Denver used to run an Ikea delivery service, where they took Ikea orders online, then shopped for and delivered the furniture.

Here's the point: the glory of living in your calling doesn't come without the grind of working in some not-so-glamorous positions.

the glory of living in your calling doesn't
come without the grind of working in
some not-so-glamorous positions.

If your dream or calling or church plant can't support you full time upfront, don't be discouraged. Get what you can and focus as much as you can on your calling. God will honor your diligence as you do what you need to do to take care of your family.

While you're at it crushing that tent making work, beware of subtle spiritual attack. It was during my tentmaking days as a janitor that Satan began attacking me in a unique way. In the past, attacks had come in the form of temptation, distractions, and outright sin. But I had pushed through those. We had sold a lot of our belongings and taken the bold step of launching out across the country. Now we lived in Clarksville and were putting roots down in the city we believed God had called us to. So Satan, being the sneaky snake he is, switched tactics. He's constantly on the prowl like a roaring lion, and when one tactic doesn't work, he'll switch to one that does. Since I didn't have time for the temptations and distractions that he used against me before, he started using pats on the back and positive encouragement instead. As I swept and mopped floors late at night, I began hearing him tell me things like, "You deserve so much more than this." "You've worked too hard to be here doing such menial tasks." "Don't settle for this dumb job. You're creative. You could make so much more money elsewhere."

I wish I could say I pulled a Nehemiah every time and rebuked his devilish lies, but I didn't. Sometimes I would start to listen to the voices. I would begin to believe the lies that I deserved more and that this was a waste of time. After all, did I really think God moved me across the country to polish floors and shine windows? No! I came to plant a church and share the Gospel...or did I? I knew that planting a church was the main objective, but deep down, I knew it would be a process. I had known this would be hard, but the church hadn't even started and it was already this hard?!

Those first weeks, months, and years are hard, but they're so good. You're learning so much even when you don't realize it. God doesn't owe you a full-time spot on a church staff. In fact, He doesn't owe you a paycheck at all. Be thankful for the role you get to play and work hard in that job while you have it. Here's how Titus put it:

> **"Bondservants are to be submissive to their own masters in everything; they are to be well-pleasing, not argumentative, not pilfering, but showing all good faith, so that in everything they may adorn the doctrine of God our Savior." (Titus 2:9–10 ESV)**

In our day, we can substitute "employee" where it says "bondservant" and "boss" where it says "master." Titus says that the whole reason we should work our jobs in a way that is well-pleasing, not argumentative, not pilfering, and in good faith is so we may "adorn the doctrine of God our Savior." Working hard makes the Gospel look good to those who are watching.

—— 99 ——

Working hard makes the Gospel look
good to those who are watching.

After all, if you're a slacker on the job, why would your coworkers or employers want anything to do with this "good news" you're peddling?

WINSOME TO WIN SOME

I didn't move to Clarksville to mop floors, drive buses, or design logos, but it's what I had to do to make things work, so I tried to make the best of it. I figured if the Apostle Paul could write a book about joy as a prisoner in a Roman prison cell, I could have joy as a substitute school bus driver. Paul put it this way:

> **"I want you to know, brothers, that what has happened to me has really served to advance the gospel, so that it has become known throughout the whole imperial guard and to all the rest that my imprisonment is for Christ."**
> **(Philippians 1:12–13 ESV)**

Those verses stopped me in my tracks when I read them in my first few weeks as a bus driver. If Paul's imprisonment was "for Christ" and could "advance the gospel," the same could be true of driving a school bus or shipping coffee or designing CD layouts. Paul was chained to Roman guards, so he had a captive audience. Literally. I had another bus driver with me during my first few months of training, which became my version of an audience. If it could "become known throughout the whole imperial guard" that Paul's chains were in Christ, I figured it could become known throughout the whole Clarksville Montgomery County School System transportation department that my driving and work ethic were in Christ. As I drove students around, often accompanied by another driver, I prayed, struck up conversations with them, invited people to church, and so much more. I realized that I had come to reach people in Clarksville and God had strategically paired them up with me, whether they liked it or not.

If Paul became a Jew to win Jews or as one under the law to win those under the law (1 Corinthians 9 ESV), then I could become a bus driver to win bus drivers. You can do the same in your own area of expertise.

Become a barista to win baristas and coffee drinkers.

Become a banker to win bankers and bank customers.

Become a waiter to win the waitstaff and customers you serve.

Become an Uber driver to drive people to their jobs and to Jesus.

Soak in your time working in the non-church world, surrounded by people who need Jesus. If you're a church planter, you will most likely eventually be full time at a church surrounded by Christians and you'll have to work at making friends who don't know Jesus.

Whatever I do, I want my attitude and work ethic to provide a platform for the gospel. However many jobs you juggle and wherever you work, make that your goal: be winsome so you can win some!

Work hard, but don't forget to play hard too...

Be winsome so you can win some!

WORK HARD, BUT NOT TOO HARD

Have you ever cried because your lawn looked so good? I'm not proud of it, but I have. That should have been a sign that I was too stressed.

I had let my grass go for too long already, and I knew I was heading home after a full day of driving buses and working the warehouse to a three-hour mowing, sweating, mosquito-bitten nightmare. After all, there was a reason our landlord had left their lawnmowers behind. I often had to rotate mowers since one would normally give out halfway through, so I'd bring in the pinch hitter to finish the job. Sunset was approaching and my window of daylight was quickly closing. As I sped home from a long day of work, I could already smell the grass cuttings and feel the sweat dripping and my future mosquito bites itching. As I took a left onto our street, I dreaded the sight I would see as I pulled up. Then to my surprise, I realized my lawn looked amazing. Shockingly good, actually. Was I looking at the right house? What happened? Had God deployed a lawn-mowing angel to meet my needs that day? I quickly parked my truck in the driveway and got out to admire the yard, standing there, awestruck with my hands on my hips. This was professional work. Next-level lawn mowing. As I got to the edge of the lawn, Jenn walked out with a smile on her face. As I turned toward her, one single solitary tear rolled down my cheek. "Who did this?!" I asked, relieved and amazed. "A guy knocked on the door and asked if we needed the lawn mowed, but I turned him down because it was going to cost $40," she said. "But then I decided it would be worth it because I knew how much you were dreading it, so I chased him down and he came back and mowed." I've always been attracted to my wife, but I was suddenly even more attracted in that moment (insert heart-eyes emoji here). I hugged her and thanked her...and realized I was losing my mind.

The weight of balancing work, ministry, a growing team, a newly acquired lease agreement, kids, a marriage, a new community, and many other things rumbling around your head like a washing machine is often overwhelming. I've seen church planters and well-meaning, faithful Christians filled with excitement and promise drop off the map, leave their families, and lose their minds. If you don't show your calendar who is boss, it will show you who's boss, and it won't be pretty. Guard time for your family (something I'm still working hard at ten years in), and most importantly guard time with the Lord. Your relationship with Him is more than just building a church. What does it profit you if you gain a megachurch with nine locations and lose your soul? If you lose your marriage, you lose your ministry. It's not worth it.

What does it profit you if you gain a megachurch with nine locations and lose your soul?

Those early days are often some of the hardest. We had some friends visit us for Awaken's first birthday in September 2010. They had talked and prayed about moving to Clarksville to help with the church, but I think our honest assessment of the challenge of that first year may have scared them away from it. Like we discussed in Chapter 1, church planting isn't for everyone. Year one was really hard. I regularly felt exhausted. There were a couple times when Jenn or I had to sit down with each other and say, "This isn't working," then figure out what needed to change and where to go from there.

Lifelong ministry and faithfulness to your family doesn't happen by accident. You have to pace yourself. Guard your time off. Leave the office early when you can. Schedule date nights with your spouse and time off with your kids. Take weekends off and weeks away periodically. My days off are Fridays and Saturdays, and I love them! Find a schedule that works for you and make sure you guard time off. As a pastor, you'll have to work hard at training up other teachers in your place, but it will be worth your investment. Not only do I train up teachers in house, but I like to budget to bring in guest speakers too. The church gets blessed and I get de-stressed. Win-win! A pastor friend of mine only taught about half of the weekends last year and spread the rest out between other local pastors and a few guest speakers. His marriage is strong and his five kids love Jesus and love church. There's a strong correlation with his commitment to them and their love for him and for Jesus. There's also a reason he has five kids, if you know what I mean!

(SUPER)NATURAL PROVISION

In 1 Kings 17, the prophet Elijah crosses paths with a widow who has one meal left. She's about to make dinner for herself and her son then starve to death. That was it for them. Then Elijah rolled onto the scene. He gave her a word from the Lord then challenged her faith by telling her to make him some food first! The audacity! Maybe chivalry is dead. She and her son were about to die anyway. Or were they?

Elijah makes a bold promise: "'The jar of flour shall not be spent, and the jug of oil shall not be empty, until the day that the Lord sends rain upon the earth'" (1 Kings 17:14 ESV).

She trusted the Lord and He proved Himself. "The jar of flour was not spent, neither did the jug of oil become empty, according to the word of the Lord that he spoke by Elijah" (1 Kings 17:16 ESV).

Early in our time in Clarksville, Jenn read that story in her daily time with the Lord and she couldn't seem to get past it. She said every day it was like the Lord would take her back to that story. She kept asking God what the message was. Eventually it became clear: we were in the famine and God was asking us to trust Him with the little bit of oil and flour we had left.

In the first two years of living in Clarksville, with all of my jobs and random income combined, I never made quite enough to pay our bills. There were times when things felt pretty desperate. I remember a couple times in particular when Jenn and I had enough money in our bank account to buy groceries for the next couple of weeks and that was it. There were a few times we literally got on our knees and prayed for God to provide miraculously for our family.

We put Him to the test and He came through just like He said He would.

Rain was God's natural means of provision for the widow and her son. A reliable paycheck was God's natural means of provision for us.

But when the natural means of provision ran dry, God promised to provide supernaturally.

Like that widow made meals for some time with the little left in her jar, somehow we paid our bills every month with the little we had in our account. I believe God honored my commitment to work hard, provide for my family, and trust Him through it all.

The good news is that when you are hard at work living in your calling, it will grab people's attention. There's something contagious about someone who loves what they do and gives it their all. As you work hard at what God has called you to, you'll be amazed at the team that begins to surround you.

God honors work and He honors faith. Work hard, but remember Who the Provider really is.

FIVE
BYE BYE, MIKE WAZOWSKI

Fight for unity and diversity.

Mike Wazowski.

If you're a parent or a twenty-something, you know who I'm talking about. He's the scrawny, cyclops-like monster from *Monsters, Inc*. He's predominately an eyeball with scrawny arms, legs, hands, and feet. He is a memorable character and simultaneously/unfortunately, a visual of how a lot of churches end up being structured these days: mainly made up of and focused on one body part. Paul warned us about that in his first letter to the Corinthians, telling us of the importance of empowering and appreciating all the spiritual gifts within the church. We all have to work hard against our tendency to surround ourselves with people who look and talk and work just like we do.

When we aren't gifted in a certain way, we tend to overlook the importance of that gift within the church. Think of it like the love languages. Gary Chapman's book, *The Five Love Languages*, helps you learn some of the primary ways we give and receive love. The interesting thing about it is that typically, the way you receive love is the way you give love. For instance, my primary love language is physical touch, and my wife's is acts of service. If I came home and the house was dirty, but Jenn greeted me with a kiss, and hugged me and told me she missed me, I'm good. I couldn't care less about some cluttered counters. I'm a happy husband. Since I feel loved that way, I have a tendency to think everyone feels love in the same way. Not the case. If Jenn came home and the house was a mess, and I just wanted to hug and kiss her, she wouldn't be able to focus on a kiss because the counters are making too much noise! To her, I've never been sexier than when I'm doing dishes or vacuuming the stairs. Hold that thought. I think I have some dusting to do...

How we receive love tends to be the way we give love. The trick is, not everyone receives it the same way. Similar to how we tend to develop tunnel vision for our personal love language, we can do the same with our spiritual gifts. We have a tendency to view our gifting as "more important" and the gifts of others as less important. Having a high view of what God has gifted you with is a good thing, but having a low view of the other gifts within the church can be disastrous.

BURGERS AND BIBLES

Four large boxes of hot dogs and frozen burger patties? Check.

Ice, cases of soda, and Capri Suns in a massive ice chest? Check.

Poster board signs that resemble a middle school science fair project? You know it.

We knew next to nothing about starting a church when we arrived in Clarksville. The best strategy we knew was go to the people ready to serve. That's a good principle, but we executed it very poorly.

We located eight local parks, printed flyers that we distributed around town, then on the first Saturday night, we loaded up my green 1997 Toyota Tacoma with all the goods. We were ready to feed hundreds of people.

Two families showed up. Not two hundred. Two. We had more people on our "launch team" (if you could call it that) than showed up on that first night at the park.

"Did you get enough to eat?" I asked everyone a few times. "Go back for seconds, thirds, and nineteenths if you'd like!"

Here is the original Awaken Church launch plan in nine words:

Hit the ground running and hope for the best.

Not the best strategy, I admit. I still laugh when I look back on those first few weeks and months, our heads spinning with questions and our wheels spinning trying to gain traction.

Jenn and I sold our house and car in May 2009, moved to Clarksville in June, started weekly park outreaches in July, launched a home Bible study in August, and opened the church doors in September.

We hit the ground running and kept up that breakneck pace for awhile.

No interest meetings.

No launch team prep.

No training.

No fundraising.

Just a crazy cocktail of vision, faith, and naivety.

Although I don't recommend that as a launch strategy (I use that phrase lightly), I hope our lack of preparation encourages you. If you have even thought about the things I mentioned, you are already ahead of where we started! There are plenty of things you could never plan for, so plan for what you can and trust God to carry you through the rest.

The church functions as a team, a family. We all have a role to play and responsibilities to fulfill.

The church functions as a team, a family. We all have a role to play and responsibilities to fulfill. The sooner you find your area and empower others for theirs, the better the church will run and the more efficiently you will be able to reach people.

BETTER TOGETHER

"Thanks, but I think I'm good."

That was my naive, dismissive response to a CPA from our church when I announced we were leaving soon to plant a church. He volunteered to help get our church plant established as a 501(c)3 organization, help write our bylaws, and a bunch of other things I had no idea about that I was sure I didn't need help with.

The legalities of church planting were some of the furthest things from my mind at the beginning. Vision, passion, Bible teaching, evangelism... those were the things I wanted to focus on. After all, those are the things God is focused on, right? Yes, but there's a catch.

Reaching people requires resources.

Resources require stewardship.

Stewardship requires faithfulness (see 1 Corinthians 4:2 ESV).

Part of being faithful is knowing what you're doing in the first place! It's the nature of the beast.

I wish business and buildings and budgets had nothing to do with church, but if we're going to be successful in funneling resources into reaching people, buying buildings, and paying staff, we have to be good at this technical, legal, administrative side of ministry...or at least bring people around us who are.

Just because I don't prefer dealing with the business side of the church doesn't mean it will go away. In fact, if I ignore it, the church I've worked so hard to build may be the thing that goes away!

Back to that CPA...

"Hey! About that offer you made me a while back... I think I could use some help after all." Once I came to my senses and realized I had a professional CPA offering to help me be legal and setup for success, I jumped at the opportunity. Here's the cool part: I asked him to join my board as a legality at first, but he's turned into one of the longest-lasting and most influential board members I have. I've flown him to Clarksville a handful of times over the years, he's helped us with hiring, strategizing, and even undoing situations we got ourselves into. Awaken is ten years running, and I couldn't be more thankful for his help and influence. The right people in the right places are worth their weight in gold (which should be accounted for, budgeted, and reported to the IRS, by the way!).

If you're like me, the business side of church is boring and over your head. That's the beauty of the church body. We can do exponentially more together than we ever could alone! Whatever God leads you to step into, you will need others to help you pull it off successfully. Like the NFL Draft, you have to be very strategic with who you place onto your team.

We can do exponentially more together than we ever could alone!

PASS THE BABY

Since our launch strategy was virtually nonexistent, our small team wore many hats in the beginning of the church. When Awaken launched, Nate was the setup team, sound engineer, and security. Denver tag-teamed with Nate for all of his roles and also did announcements, bulletin printing, maintenance, and often helped with kids ministry. Jenn, Nate's wife, having never served in a kids ministry before and without children of her own, for some reason seemed to be the natural choice to launch and oversee the kids ministry. My wife, Jenn, was our worship leader, bookkeeper, mother of one (soon to be two, now three), and her hardest job, wife to Kevin Miller. Once she gave birth to our second daughter four weeks after launch and took a month off of leading worship, she dove right back in. Since our daughter wouldn't let anyone else besides us touch her, while Jenn led worship, I would hold Adalyn in the back. As Jenn finished and people shook hands, I would pass Adalyn off in the middle of the aisle as Jenn put down her guitar and walked to the back and I walked to the front to preach. Sundays were another story for the first five or so years as Jenn left early for worship rehearsal and I tried to wrap my head around my sermon for the final time while I wrangled our two daughters, got them dressed, fed them breakfast, and attempted to defrazzle their hair.

In 2016, as Jenn left early on a Saturday morning for worship rehearsal, she was in a brutal collision. A girl ran a stoplight, t-boning Jenn directly in the driver's side door of our Toyota Tacoma, pushing the truck through the intersection and almost rolling it over. Our truck was totaled, but Jenn was protected. Over the following months as Jenn slowly recovered, thoughts of life and ministry without her periodically flashed through my mind. I had to quickly banish them from my head as the thought of going on without her is unimaginable.

Although God has called each one of us individually to step into something unique, when He pairs us with a spouse, he or she becomes an inseparable part of that calling. Although our first decade of church planting has been some of the wildest and hardest years of our lives, there is no one better to be in it with than the one and only Jenn Miller. She lives with integrity, leads with humility, and loves unconditionally. I consider it one of the highest honors of my life to be her husband.

I didn't write this section to earn brownie points with my wife (although speaking of my wife and brownies... have you tried her triple chocolate espresso brownies?!) or an endorsement from Hallmark. I wrote it as a reminder of the beauty of pursuing your calling with someone else. This chapter is about a team and I haven't always valued the team as I should. Whether your entire team lives under your roof or grows to dozens or hundreds under many roofs, never underestimate the importance of the people God has placed in your life.

I learned early on that as long as I am unwilling to empower others and train them in the work of the ministry, I am the lid to the growth of our church or ministry. The church can only carry the weight that the combined shoulders of your team is able to bear. The more weight-bearing shoulders that are available, the more people you can collectively reach.

The church can only carry the weight that the combined shoulders of your team is able to bear. The more weight-bearing shoulders that are available, the more people you can collectively reach.

EVERYBODY NEEDS A NATE

Speaking of a team, I can't go on without talking about another indispensable part of the Awaken Church team, Nate. I met Nate Witiuk (pronounced "Witt-ick" or if you're Siri, "Widdy-yuck") about a year and a half before we left Albuquerque for Clarksville. He was finishing up his college degree at the time and looking for a place to serve, so youth ministry it was! He and I hit it off right away and in addition to helping me around the office and leading worship for the youth group periodically, he and I became fast friends. Whether it was movie nights while our wives were away or Nate and his wife, Jenn, introducing us to their favorite Ukrainian cuisine, pierogies, we just clicked. Little did I know that God was planting the seeds of friendship in order to grow a ministry partnership that would change both of our lives and thousands of others.

As Nate and I watched a few groups of our friends go out to

plant churches, he periodically asked if Jenn and I were going to follow suit. Although I wasn't in a place to advertise my departure, as I started to recognize the call and plans began falling into place, it became clear I needed to share the news with him.

I asked him to grab coffee one afternoon, a meeting he thought had to do with a youth group mission trip I was having him lead. Nope. Different mission trip.

In a now-closed coffee shop on Paseo Del Norte and Louisiana Blvd. in Albuquerque, NM, Nate became the first person I shared our exciting departure news with.

I told him, "I'm not inviting you to come with us; I'm just telling you our plans to plant a church." He looked at me, somewhat shocked, then said, "Well, it looks like Jenn and I are planting a church too." And just like that, our church planting team doubled in size from one couple to two!

That's the kind of loyalty Nate lives out. Our wives made one trip to Clarksville a few months before the final move in order to nail down housing, but Nate couldn't join due to a work commitment. The first time Nate entered the state of Tennessee was when he rolled into Clarksville in their moving truck, carrying all of their earthly possessions, including their dog, Matilda. Tennessee is called "The Volunteer State," and I guess he took that literally!

From the beginning, Nate has been willing to do whatever it takes to get the job done. He got an internship at an insurance company in Nashville when he first moved to Clarksville, requiring an hour-long daily commute. He would get off at 5:00 pm, drive his Infiniti faster than he should to get to the church by 6:00 pm, often still wearing his tie, and help with last-minute prep for our Wednesday night services. He would do whatever it took and work as hard as was needed to make things happen.

To this day, I can't imagine leading the church without him. I often joke that he runs the church and I just show up and teach, but I'm only partly joking. He and I are wired very differently, yet we compliment each other well. He helps ground me and I help stretch him. He has this unique, God-given, MacGyver-style ability to defuse potentially explosive situations with a laugh and a smile. He's not a "yes" man and we have disagreed about a lot over the years, but we've remained united, pressing forward through some really hard times.

If you're a Lead Pastor, pray for a Nate. You can't have mine - he's taken.

If you're not a Lead Pastor, be a Nate. Support, encourage, and execute the vision. The supporting role you play is as vital to your pastor as Aaron and Hur were to Moses' weary arms. Your role, although different from his, is just as important in winning the war and building the church.

SAY "NO" TO A "YES TEAM"

Speaking of Nate, someone once seemed to infer that Nate just goes along with what I say without questioning as though I hired him to be my "yes man." I had to laugh at that. If only people had a peek into the weekly meetings I have with him and other pastors as well as our monthly Pastors and Overseers meetings. We regularly disagree on things: what to name ministries, when to plan certain events, who to hire, how and where to invest the church's finances, and more. We don't argue about them, but we certainly don't agree on everything. As it turns out, some disagreement and discussion is actually a really healthy thing.

Nate and the other Pastors have different vantage points. By speaking up and voicing our opinions and thoughts, we often help to cover each other's blindspots.

Differing viewpoints are necessary in life and ministry.

For instance, sometimes when I'm driving and about to make a left turn across a few lanes of traffic, I'll ask my wife if it's clear from her vantage point on the passenger side. When I ask her that, I do not want her to tell me it's clear because she thinks I want to hear that. If I pull out into oncoming traffic and get t-boned by a car she didn't tell me was there, I don't want her justification to be, "Well, I knew you were in a hurry and wanted to get home quickly, so I told you the traffic was clear to make you happy." If she gives me a "yes" when it should have been a "no" or at least a "not yet," she could not only make us even later than we would have been, but she could cost us a lot of money or even our lives! I need her honest perspective. Since she has a different vantage point as a passenger, she is able to help cover my blindspot. She can see things I can't and give valuable feedback that can greatly improve our chances of safely arriving at our destination.

The same is true for the team you have around you.

If you surround yourself with "yes" men (or women), they will regularly say "yes" when they should be saying "no," causing you to inadvertently pull out into oncoming traffic. Best case scenario, there will be some swerving, squealing brakes, and close misses. Worst case scenario, the results of surrounding yourself with a "yes" team could be catastrophic to you personally as well as corporately to the church you lead.

What we all need is a team of Micaiahs.

Micaiah was a prophet to the nation of Israel at the time of King Ahab. King Ahab is fired up and ready to head into war, and as a show of spirituality, he gathers his team of "yes" men around him, asking if he should go into battle. 1 Kings 22:6 ESV says that his team enthusiastically replied, "Go up, for the Lord will give it into the hand of the king." They knew what he wanted to hear, and as his faithful and loyal "yes" men (I feel weird using "faithful" and "loyal" to describe these devious men), they replied with the only word they knew how to tell him: "YES!" After all, he's the king. He should do what he wants to do and no one should be able to stop him.

King Jehoshaphat, King of Judah, who Ahab had asked to join him in war, being a wise and God-fearing king, asked if there were any other prophets they could speak to. Cue Micaiah. He's locked up in a prison cell at the time, but they head out to get him at the king's request...but not without some coaching first. The messenger tells Micaiah that everyone else has spoken favorably toward the king, so it would be in Micaiah's best interest to do the same. Translation: "Just tell the king 'yes,' and everything will be much smoother for you." You need to read the story for yourself after this, as it's quite the scene of sarcasm, visions, truth, a punch to the face, and Micaiah being dragged back to prison after telling Ahab "no," something no one dared to do.

Ahab went to battle anyway, pulling out into oncoming traffic when Micaiah had warned him not to, leading to an epic, bloody end to his life. (I'll spare you the details about dogs, blood, and prostitutes, but the Bible doesn't spare you!)

Why the sudden, tragic, unnecessary end? He was surrounded by "yes" men. They were not willing to cross him even when telling him no was the right thing to do.

Here's one more warning: surrounding yourself with "yes" men is your natural default mode. It's mine too. It's not natural to surround yourself with people who will challenge your decisions, talk you through things, and regularly state their opinions (all of which should be done with humility and loyalty to the vision, by the way). Our natural instinct is to surround ourselves with the guys like Ahab surrounded himself: people who make you feel good and help you get your way.

Instead of a "yes" team, surround yourself with a P.R.A.Y. team. Your P.R.A.Y. team will help you consider four important things:

Priorities

Always consider this first. Does the decision you're considering match the vision, direction, and priorities of your life, ministry, family, and calling? This must be the primary, prayerful consideration in any decision.

Risk

Since I am a "big vision" guy, I need people to help me think through the risk and the real-world consequences of my decisions. Who will this decision affect if it fails or succeeds, and how will it affect them? Is the price tag too big if it were to fail?

Ability

It may be the best idea you've ever had, but is it realistic? Obviously, if God is calling you to it, He'll equip you for it, but a realistic look at your ability, as well as your team's and your church's ability is important. Is it in the budget or should we make it fit the budget? Is right now the time to pull the trigger? Can our team support this?

Yours

Is this decision or plan right for *you*? There are thousands of legitimate needs, campaigns, organizations, and charities to start and support, but is this one yours to focus on? Has God called you to it *right now*? Not every need has your name on it. "No" is a powerful, clarifying, empowering, underutilized word.

Make sure your P.R.A.Y. team is made up of humble, servant-hearted, loyal, prayerful people. They're not in it for themselves; they're in it for God, for you, and for the vision of the church. This team is indispensable to your success in life and ministry.

DO NOT BE UNI(N)FORMED

"The Austin Peay State University football team will be at church this Sunday," my assistant told me over the phone with only a few days left until Sunday. "I just got a phone call from one of the coaches and he said they're bringing the entire team, so there will be between eighty and ninety players and their coaches."

For some large churches, that wouldn't be too much of an issue. However, our venues seat 110 each, so ninety first-time guests is almost the equivalent of adding in the attendance of a third venue of the same size!

We spread the word via our teams and social media and we made room for about ninety guys, most of them weighing between 200-300 pounds and standing six feet or taller.

What I loved about it was the diversity. It's not that our church isn't diverse; we actually get a lot of compliments about that. It's just that when you bring in a football team, you notice the diversity of your church (or lack thereof) a lot more.

A football team is actually a great picture of how God designed the church to be. Every player has a unique role on the team, but although their roles are unique, their mission is the same: win. In the midst of their diversity (skin color, position, height and weight), they are united under the same coach, against the same enemy, heading in the same direction.

The church has a lot to learn from football teams.

Thankfully the fight for unity in the midst of diversity isn't unique to modern Christianity. It goes back to our roots. Paul wrote about it a couple thousand years ago when he addressed the Corinthian church. He told them, "Concerning spiritual gifts, brothers, I do not want you to be uninformed" (1 Cor 12:1 ESV).

"Now there are varieties of gifts, but the same Spirit; and there are varieties of service, but the same Lord; and there are varieties of activities, but it is the same God who empowers them all in everyone. To each is given the manifestation of the Spirit for the common good."
(1 Corinthians 12:4-7 ESV)

Did you pick up on that unity in the midst of their diversity? We are many, but we are also one.
We do many things, but we primarily do one thing.

"

We are many, but we are also one.
We do many things, but we primarily
do one thing.

He wrote this letter to them because he said he didn't want them to be *uninformed,* but if you remove the second "n" from that word, it proves his other point. Even though it was the same God, the same Lord, the same Spirit behind their service, Paul appreciated variety — in gifts, service, and activities. He didn't want them *uninformed,* but he also didn't want them to be *uniformed*—all doing the same thing the same way.

You know uniforms, especially if you have to wear one for your job. Baseball players, the hotel concierge, and the employees at Hot Dog on a Stick all understand. And speaking of the employees of your favorite fast food corn dog establishment, Hot Dog on a Stick, God bless them! I have a theory that if you trace the history of their company back far enough, you'll find that their giant, multi-colored hats and goofy fabric shorts began as a prank or a drunken dare and somehow got drafted into the employee handbook. Or maybe someone lost a bet. I can't explain how those outfits became the mandatory dress, but more power to them for rocking them with pride! There are a lot of things you can pay me to do, but wear that outfit is not one of them (says the former janitor who fell asleep in the women's dressing room).

Being uninformed is almost as dangerous as being uniform. Unfortunately, uniformity is our natural tendency. Just look around. America likes to claim that racism is a thing of the past, but we are fooling ourselves if we believe that! I shudder every time I hear a local pastor refer to their church as a "black church" or a "white church." Revelation says that people of every tribe, nation, people, and tongue will be worshiping Jesus in heaven. We should fight hard to give people a taste of that diversity on this side of heaven!

Not only should our skin colors be diverse, but God designed the church to be diverse in its gifts, services, and activities. If we are going to see this Biblical diversity throughout the church, it has to start from the top.

Our pastoral team at Awaken is very diverse. At the time of

this writing, I have a team of four pastors (including me) and three pastors-in-training that we call Overseers.

I bring fifteen years of pastoral ministry experience to the team.

Nate's ministry experience is the entire ten-year history of Awaken Church.

Jim was a pastor for twenty-five years and now works in the corporate world.

Divone went to ministry school and has a business degree. He spent a few years in the Army, has been a pastor for about three years, and now works in the real estate world as a loan officer.

Josh spent a few years in the Army and now works as a financial advisor.

Seth went to West Point and plans to retire from the Army by the age of forty so he can focus on ministry full-time.

Jason just recently joined the leadership team and is currently working as a manager at a local networking and computer company.

Why do I mention all of that? Because it has taken years of hard work and intentionality on my part and the part of other leaders to ensure we have a diverse team. Although the seven of us work well together and fight hard for unity, I would be lying if I said we always agree on things. Even over the last year, we have struggled as we have fought to continue building a diverse, unified team. We have seen people come and go and at times, I have wondered if our team would work for the long term. Although we will not all be together serving for the rest of our lives, we pray and fight for unity while protecting our diversity, understanding that we are in some ways a microcosm of the rest of the church.

If your leadership and staff are not diverse, you cannot expect the rest of the church to be. And if diversity is something you don't like, you are going to hate heaven!

If your leadership and staff are not diverse, you cannot expect the rest of the church to be. And if diversity is something you don't like, you are going to hate heaven!

Although there are many ways people can serve within the church and as leaders, integrity is a non-negotiable. You cannot afford to say no to integrity in the name of diversity.

INTEGRITY OVER ABILITY

They say "teamwork makes the dream work," and I concur. Planting and building a church was always meant to be a team sport, not a solo campaign built around the talent of one. As Pastor Brian Houston puts it, "Church is not built on the gifts and talents of a few, but on the sacrifices of many."[1]

Although that is true, you'll be tempted to try to build your church on the talents of a few, yourself included. It's easy to see someone who is extraordinarily gifted in what they do and rely far too heavily on them. At Awaken, we aim to always choose integrity over ability. Don't get me wrong, talent and ability are important. You don't want someone leading worship who would make it onto the bloopers of *American Idol* tryouts, William Hung style ("She bang! She bang!"). God cared about talent and ability; just read about Bezalel in Exodus 31 ESV. God specifically gifted Bezalel and Oholiab with ability, intelligence, knowledge, and craftsmanship. He didn't want just any Joe Shmoe with a hammer and a sewing needle out there building the tabernacle and sewing the curtains. In fact, part of His instructions for the curtains in the tabernacle were that they should be made "skillfully" (Exodus 26:1 ESV). No matter how skillful Bezalel was, the first thing on the list of what made him the right guy for the job was that he was filled with the Spirit of God (Exodus 31:3 ESV). God cares much more about integrity than He does about ability. In fact, it was multiple breaches of integrity that caused God to rip the kingdom from the white-knuckled grip of a massively able King, Saul. Ability? Absolutely. Integrity? Not at all.

God cares much more about integrity
than He does about ability.

The last thing you want is a team member who is super talented, but living a morally compromising life. Not only will that sin (gossip, pride, lust, infidelity, unfaithfulness, etc.) eat away at them and cause them to quit early, but it will become poison on your team and in your future church. Believe me, you will have enough problems to face when launching the church! You need the least amount of problems from your team. Integrity is vital; ability is trainable. We have hired a handful of staff that didn't fit all of our desired qualifications for the job, but that were humble, teachable, driven, and called.

For the last year or so, I've been compiling a list of people I see faithfully serving around our church that I think may fit somewhere on our staff in the future. I write them in my prayer journal, and as I thumb through it, I'll often pray for them by name, asking for God's timing and will if they are to join our team. I remember the first time that list got put to use. I was surprised to hear one of our staff members was taking a job elsewhere. It seemed like a setback at first until I thought of one of the people I had been praying for for a couple weeks. "Sara!" I said, excitedly, after a minute of thinking about what our next move would be. "I have a list of potential future staff I've been praying for and Sara is one of them. I've been waiting for an opportunity to hire her!" Interestingly, she was the same one our team had already been talking about to fill the slot that had just opened. Just a few weeks later on Sara's first day on the team, I loved being able to tell her she was an answer to prayer!

When you find someone with a high standard of integrity and who is willing to work hard and serve wherever is needed, hold on and don't let go!

Teamwork may make the dream work, but don't overlook the One who gave the dream to begin with...

Teamwork may make the dream work,
but don't overlook the One who gave
the dream to begin with...

EVEN MORE IMPORTANT THAN A TEAM

I remember the moment I knew we were going to make it.

I had been panicked up until then. I had seen a couple other prospective planters leave already, taking a dozen or more people with them. They had team worship nights, team building activities, team dinners, and other team-themed events. It turns out the prerequisite for having a team event is having a team, and I didn't have one. Well, I guess I did, if you count my wife, our two-year old, and our in-utero baby. I knew for sure they were going with me. They had to.

The other guys who were heading out to plant had the luxury of telling anyone and everyone they met that they were leaving and wanted them to come with them. Talk about recruiting! Their conversations went something like, "Man, it's a hot day, huh? You know where it's not hot and actually has an amazing climate, a great economy, a low crime rate, and has been rated one of the top cities to raise a family? The place I'm going to plant a church! You and your family and all your neighbors should come with us!"

Since I was the youth pastor at the time, I didn't have the same luxury of campaigning for my 2009 run as a church planter. My pastor had asked me not to spread the word until we knew who would be replacing me, and we still didn't know for sure. So there they went, snatching up all the prospective launch team members while I faithfully taught middle schoolers, pretending like I wasn't leaving in a few months. People periodically told me they were praying about planting a church with the next up-and-coming church planter. I would encourage them or celebrate with them, secretly wondering when I'd be on the other side of the conversation and if there would be anyone left when I was.

It was a frustrating season for me, but my frustration was self-inflicted. I was crying about a weight I had taken out of God's hands and tried to drag along by myself. It's like when my five-year old son insists on doing the work himself, carrying a box that's too big for him or lifting a dumbbell that's too heavy for him. He's stubbornly independent (I'm not sure where he got that from) and regularly refuses to do something unless we take our hands off and give him complete control.

I do that with God more than I care to admit. Not only do I end up carrying a weight I was not meant to carry, but I also end up complaining about the weight I am carrying that I should not have been carrying to begin with.

Back to that moment I mentioned when I knew we would make it...

I was sitting on the front row, listening to my pastor teach the Bible as I had for the last five years. No one around me knew of the inner turmoil I was facing, even him. He knew about my plans to plant, but had no idea of the doubt I was dealing with. I'm not sure what the sermon was about that day, but I know it was meant for me. I was just one of the 10,000+ people in one of four weekend services that weekend, but it was like the message was intended just for me. God has a way of specifically speaking to us if we will just listen. I don't know if he was teaching from Exodus 33 or just mentioned it for part of the message, but I immediately connected with it. Exodus 33 begins with God sending Moses out to a new location to lead His people, which sounded oddly familiar and personal to me. I'd like to say I relate to Moses because our large dose of humility, but it's probably more accurate to say I relate to him via his insecurities and doubt. As God commissioned Moses, I was intrigued to read that Moses was dealing with the same questions I was currently wrestling with.

In Exodus 33, Moses tells God,

"See, you say to me, 'Bring up this people,' but you have not let me know whom you will send with me. Yet you have said, 'I know you by name, and you have also found favor in my sight. Now therefore, if I have found favor in your sight, please show me now your ways, that I may know you in order to find favor in your sight. Consider too that this nation is your people.'" (Exodus 33:12-13 ESV)

Translation: "God, you're sending me out to lead Your people, but I don't have a team. If you really love me, and since these are Your people, not mine, tell me the plan."

"YES!" I screamed (in my mind). That is exactly it! One of my Bible heroes wrestled with the same question I was wrestling with, and God used him for great things! His calling was similar to mine and his question was similar to mine, so I couldn't wait to read the next verse about God's response and the massive team of skilled, talented, world-changers God was going to promise to Moses (and to me)! So I kept reading…

"And he said, 'My presence will go with you, and I will give you rest'" (Exodus 33:14 ESV).

That was not what I expected, but it was all I needed. In that moment, on the front row of the sanctuary, God defeated my doubt and worry with His peace. My friends who had backed out, the people I didn't have the liberty to ask, the lack of campaigning and promoting... God knew all of that and had a plan anyway. If nobody else went with us, God Himself was going with us. His presence would be enough!

Promote the gifts, but don't forget the Giver of the gifts.

Pursue the dream, but don't forget the Giver of the dream.

Plant the church, but don't forget Whose church it is. Jesus bought it with His blood. We say we'll stop at nothing to build the Church, but Jesus proved that sentiment with His blood. As much as we want to see the church succeed, we'll never want it more or be as invested as Jesus.

99

As much as we want to see the church succeed, we'll never want it more or be as invested as Jesus.

NOT SO AMONG YOU

Our family got to travel to Sydney, Australia one summer. We stayed with my sister and her husband, toured the city, went whale watching, drank amazing coffee, and hit all the local hot spots like the Opera House, Luna Park, and even watched the sunset near the Sydney Harbor Bridge. One of the highlights was attending the Hillsong Conference and worshiping with 30,000 others in a stadium. We loved it heaps, mate!

Not only was attending the conference very memorable, but so was getting to and from the conference. My sister and brother-in-law were working, but took the subway so we could borrow their car during conference. Driving in the opposite side of the car on the opposite side of the road was a very unique experience. Left turns were easy, but right turns took me across multiple lanes of traffic, the opposite of how I'm accustomed to driving. Being in that culture forced me to learn a new way to drive.

Imagine my arrogance if I would have held an American flag out of my car window and drove their car on the side of the road I was accustomed to driving on. I would have put my whole family in danger and I may still have been locked up in some Aussie prison somewhere.

I can't tell you the consequences for sure, but it would not have ended well, I know that much.

The same is true for our leadership. In Mark 10, as Jesus and the disciples walk toward Jerusalem, and after James and John attempt to call dibs on Jesus' left and right hand spots in glory, Jesus uses it as a teachable moment. In this mini traveling leadership conference, He begins to point out how other worldly leaders lead from a position of fear and authority. Then Jesus tells the disciples, "Not so among you" (Mark 10:43 ESV). In other words, if we are going to lead like Jesus and build churches that accurately reflect Jesus, we are going to have to lead and build in ways that are often very contrary to how the world says to do it.

If we are going to lead like Jesus and build churches that accurately reflect Jesus, we are going to have to lead and build in ways that are often very contrary to how the world says to do it.

What we've discussed throughout this chapter flies in the face of what comes natural and what we are surrounded by in our culture. From not surrounding yourself with a yes team to fighting for diversity, choosing integrity over ability, as well as trusting God even when no one goes with you, those are all very contrary to many of the top leadership books and conferences. Jesus-style leadership feels backwards because it is. It goes against our natural, selfish tendencies as self-centered humans.

Jesus built a very diverse team of disciples that included a tax collector, some fishermen, a zealot, a backstabber, and a few other unique individuals. He built diversity, but in His final prayer before His death, He prayed for unity (John 17). He prayed we would be one as He and the Father are one. Jesus was pro-diversity and pro-unity. In that case, our leadership and our churches must reflect those same priorities.

—————————— 99 ——————————

Jesus was pro-diversity and pro-unity.
In that case, our leadership and our
churches must reflect those same
priorities.

————————————————

Jesus was a strong leader. Strong leaders inevitably face strong storms and cutting critics. You will find the same to be true as you step out in faith. Sometimes the storms will be figurative. Other times, they will be literal, like the storm we endured in the first few months after we launched...

Tropical Tanz (far right) Awaken's first location

SIX

CANOES IN THE PARKING LOT AND FISH IN THE BATHROOM

Stay anchored when the storms rage.

I say I'm a native New Mexican, but technically, I'm a native Arizonian, one of the only places drier and hotter than New Mexico. I was born in Glendale, Arizona, right outside of Phoenix. My family and I lived there until I was three, when we moved to Albuquerque, New Mexico. The only memory I have from my time in Phoenix is, "It's hot." It says a lot when you can remember anything from when you were three, so the heat must have been extreme. We eventually moved to Albuquerque, New Mexico, the Land of Enchantment (or "The Land of Entrapment" as some have affectionately termed it) and also the land of cacti, tumbleweeds, droughts, and fireworks restrictions. Flooding was not an issue in those two locations. In comparison to the river outside the front doors of our church in Clarksville, the river I grew up around, the "Rio Grande," is more like "Rio Pequeño." Muy pequeño. There are many places where you can walk all the way across it.

Fast forward to eight months into our church plant. Remember the "high water" part of the title of this book? That's not a reference to your dad's cargo pants. It's a reference to the water I was standing in, in the same spot I had preached just thirty-six hours prior.

Let's go for a walk (or a wade) down memory lane...

GOD IS NOWHERE

Awaken Church was still in its infant state in May 2010. Being that Clarksville mainly exists due to the Army influence of Ft. Campbell, the nation's second-largest Army post, our little church was greatly impacted when about half of our church took a twelve-month paid trip to Afghanistan to hunt for Osama Bin Laden and his minions. The other twenty or so of us tried to fill the gaps while our friends and family were away.

In those beginning days we had one church service on Saturday night and one on Wednesday night. Mid-deployment, a few of our Wednesday night services felt less like church and more like we had moved to Clarksville and started a fledgling women's ministry. One night in particular, I preached, Nate ran audio and video, and three women watched eighteen kids while I preached to three women, one being my wife who was also our worship leader. And you thought giving a Powerpoint presentation to your world history class was awkward!

Eight months into the church, we were struggling, but moving along as best we could. On the first Saturday night of May 2010, it rained during our entire evening service, so I preached louder than normal, making sure my voice was louder than the pounding rain. As the rain pounded the roof, the lightning and shake-the-walls thunder joined in the chorus. As services ended that night, we ducked and ran to our cars attempting in vain to avoid getting drenched. Little did we know that as we pulled out of the parking lot that night, it would be the last time we would be able to drive into the parking lot for another week. Like ministry and life, you often can't see a storm brewing until it is upon you and you don't know how bad it may get before it's over.

The shopping center that houses our church, Riverside Center, is located on Riverside Drive, about 100 feet from the Cumberland River, but the river had always done a great job at remaining in the riverbed as it should. As the rain continued through the evening and into the night, the incessant buzzing of flood warnings coming from our iPhones reminded us of the downpour happening and the danger building. It was still raining when we woke up on Sunday morning, shattering rainfall records that had been held for decades. That weekend set records for the most rainfall in six hours, twelve hours, twenty-four hours, and forty-eight hours, and May 2010 went down as the wettest month in recorded Clarksville history. Although it rained more than almost any of us had witnessed, the forecast showed a break in the clouds. By Sunday afternoon, after receiving over thirteen inches of rain in under forty-eight hours, the sun finally broke through and the rain stopped falling. Wondering how high the river was, we took a sightseeing drive through the River District. Although the locals were saying the river was higher than anyone had seen it in decades, most of the roads were still driveable, except for a few low-lying areas that were the first to flood. We drove home with a premature feeling of relief. Although the river was high, it was still mostly contained in the riverbed. Awaken Church would be just fine...or so we thought.

On Monday morning as I got ready for work, I did a double take when I saw an online picture of a Riverside Drive streetlight two blocks from Awaken. I couldn't believe my eyes. The picture showed a three-foot gap between the stoplight and the flooded river that had consumed the street below where we had driven just twelve hours prior. If the water was fifteen feet deep at that intersection, I wondered what it looked like at Riverside Center, just two blocks down!

I hurriedly jumped in my truck, trying to stay calm and not let my mind wander to worst case scenarios. As I notified my boss that I would be in late, I made the fateful drive that would be indelibly etched into my mind.

I had never seen a sight like what I saw that day in downtown Clarksville. The city was in panic mode, as though the Apocalypse had come. Gas station lines were out of the parking lots and down the streets and grocery store shelves were cleared out. Downtown, what used to be Riverside Drive was now more like River Drive, as the whole street was only accessible by boat instead of car. All of Riverside Drive was barricaded and I couldn't access our church. I drove one street north, illegally parked my truck on the side of the railroad tracks, then got out and began running.

I could have never prepared myself for the sight I would see as I ran up on our shopping center. Standing above our parking lot, overlooking Riverside Center, I couldn't see the pavement anymore. The black asphalt had been replaced with muddy, brown river water, covering the entire shopping center.

My stomach sank and my heart pounded. This was past the point of scrambling to save things; everything was already ruined. There was no undoing what had already been done.

I climbed down the thirty-foot embankment I was standing on and waded through knee-deep muddy river water to the front door of our little Awaken Church storefront, my brain struggling to process what my eyes were taking in. I fumbled for my keys in my front pocket, which was high enough to still be dry, and unlocked the glass door. I had to pull hard to open it, the resistance from a couple feet of water making the door much harder to move.

My pulpit was standing in two feet of water. The chairs that had been filled with people two days prior were now floating. A lone Bible floated down the hallway and the new drum kit someone had just donated to the church sat mostly submerged in a hall closet. I stood there, mouth open, pants and shoes soaked, eyes filling with tears, overwhelmed. It was too much to take in. What would we do now? Should we keep going? Half of our church was deployed anyway. We barely had the funds to pay rent, how would we ever be able to afford to replace what we lost? How would we be able to renovate and rebuild? I scanned the room, vision blurred and eyes stinging from tears. I counted thousands of dollars worth of chairs, floor monitors, and equipment that had been destroyed. I had uprooted my family and moved across the United States to start this church. Now it was over.

As I stared across the chairs, a banner for our teaching series through the book of Esther hanging in the distance caught my eye. We were halfway through the series we were calling "GOD IS NOWHERE," a play-on words. The book of Esther is the only book of the Bible that doesn't mention God anywhere in its pages. At first glance, like the view I was getting that morning, it appears God is nowhere to be found. But the more you dig, the more you can see God at work behind the scenes, through the tragedy. The more you stare at that banner, the more you realize it actually says "GOD IS NOW HERE." I had designed that image for our church, but now my own artwork was speaking to me.

As I stood in the same spot where I had greeted people at church just days prior, God spoke. I didn't hear an audible voice, but I know the Lord spoke to me in that moment. He reminded me, "This is My church. It has never been your church. I will build it. Trust me."

99

He reminded me, "This is My church. It
has never been your church. I will build
it. Trust me."

God is now here.

In that moment, I knew we would rebuild. The church wasn't finished.
God was just getting started. As shocked and unprepared as I felt,
God was not shocked and He was fully prepared.

I decided it was time to get to work. Come hell or *high water*,
God's church would not just survive, we would somehow thrive
through this. I took a picture with my iPhone from where I had taught
the Bible a couple days prior, looking over the floating chairs and
ever-deepening water, out into the parking lot. I posted the picture
on Facebook and got to work.

My friend Denver met me there that morning and we started
salvaging whatever we could. We took a partially submerged door
off its hinges and used it as a makeshift raft, pulling speakers off
of wall mounts, and grabbing kids ministry curriculum, the sound
board, and other things that hadn't yet been touched by the toxic
water. We double and triple trash bagged them, wading past our
floating drum kit and stack of waterlogged Bibles, loaded them
onto our makeshift life raft and floated them across the parking
spaces we had parked in two days earlier, to the hill below where
I had parked. One by one, Denver and I carried speakers and
equipment up the hill so we could load them into the back of my
truck.

In between shifts of pulling speakers up a thirty-foot grass
hill, we watched as the tenant next to us rowed a canoe across the
parking lot. We waded through to grab more gear as he loaded a
tv and some wall art into his boat and paddled toward dry ground,
past a truck someone had left parked in our parking lot that was
now flooded and floating.

After loading anything that was salvageable, we drove
away. Everything the church owned fit in a small portion of the
bed of my truck. The church owned less now than when we had
arrived in Clarksville.

That Wednesday, we met in the same living room where

we had begun meeting. It felt depressing and discouraging. Any momentum we had gained seemed to be dead, floating away with the driftwood. And yet, just as the river tide had risen, faith was rising.

The following Saturday, we and many others from around Clarksville converged on Riverside Drive. The water had receded, leaving a sticky, brown layer of foul-smelling mud on everything it had touched. Parents were advised to keep children out of the area as the water treatment plant had also flooded, pouring millions of gallons of raw sewage into the river.

As we ripped out carpet and kicked through walls, I was beckoned to the back bathroom where a fish had found its final resting place on the floor amidst the drying, cracking river mud. Out front, our destroyed chairs, cabinets, and kids toys were pushed into the middle of the parking lot into a pile that grew taller and wider by the minute. Eventually we would fill up multiple semi trucks with trash, just from the tenants in Riverside Center!

When we left that day, we had barely a shell of a building. Riverside Drive, with its piles of trash and destroyed belongings, looked like a tornado had touched down.

Through all of that ordeal, I would have never imagined I would say this next sentence: *I am thankful for the flood.* You read that right. I'm not saying I want to go through it again (although we do have flood insurance this time, just in case), and we still sweat every year when the river rises. I'm saying I am thankful for what we learned, how we grew, and how God redeemed the tragedy. It turns out He's really good at that.

Whether you plant a church, start a business, raise kids, or take any other step of faith, a forecast of storms and natural disasters is coming your way. They're guaranteed. The ride may be wet and wild, but if you're following Jesus into the storm, you can rest assured He will be with you and it will be worth it.

The ride may be wet and wild, but if you're following Jesus into the storm, you can rest assured He will be with you and it will be worth it.

THE HANDS AND FEET OF CHRIST...IN RUBBER GLOVES

One of the unexpected effects of the flood was the unity it brought. One couple, Paul and Samantha, had just come to Awaken for the first time on the weekend before the flood. On the first Saturday, they went to church. On the next Saturday - demolition day - they were the church. They rolled into the parking lot just days after the flood waters had receded with a truckload of tools, a wheelbarrow, and some extra work gloves. They reintroduced themselves to a few people, handed out tools, and got to work. It's amazing the unity that can come from kicking through walls and pulling out carpet! Tools of destruction, like sledgehammers and pry bars, became tools of unity.

Demolition and rebuilding didn't only unite a couple dozen Awaken people; it united a city. On cleanup day, people from around Clarksville converged on Riverside Drive. That was when I got to really know my friend, Carlo. At the time, He was the Young Adults Pastor at another local church. A group of young adults, who certainly had plenty of funner things to do on a Saturday than don rubber gloves and masks and rip out carpet, piled in a church van and showed up in Riverside Center ready to help. God used the flood to make new friends and cross denominational lines.

Someone donated a bunch of food and drinks that day. We drank Red Bulls and ate sub sandwiches while we sat with new friends on the curb next to a pile of our old, destroyed chairs and kids toys.

Not only did the flood bring in other local Clarksville churches, we even had friends from a church in Indiana who drove for over five hours to help us clean up and reach further into the community. We had so many people offering to help, it forced us to begin looking elsewhere to help others.

That's how we met the McLellans.

Lisa, Ron, and a small household full of four kids, all of them with special needs or handicaps, had been deeply impacted by the flooding. Their basement, where they had stored a lot of food, was flooded, destroying a lot of their stockpile. They needed hands to help, and thanks to all the volunteers that had just come into town, we had hands! A couple dozen of us came together and did in a couple hours what would have taken the McLellans days or weeks to accomplish. Their family became a vital part of our church over the next few years until they moved out of state.

All of that unity was the result of tragedy. Satan thought he was going to wipe out a church, but God used tragedy to build the Church.

———————— 99 ————————

Satan thought he was going to wipe out a church, but God used tragedy to build the Church.

S.T.E.M.

What are the odds of Awaken Church settling into Riverside Center just months before a hundred-year flood hit? No one living in Clarksville had ever seen the water as high as it was that fateful day. It hadn't been that high in decades. Before we settled into Riverside Center, we had a lease at another strip mall on much higher ground across the city. That lease fell through, which providentially led us to Riverside Drive. That was no coincidence or accident. God strategically placed us feet from the river, knowing the flood was coming, and knowing how He would use it for our good and His glory. Although the flood was tragic, our placement there was strategic.

———————— 99 ————————

God often places local churches and loving people in the midst of tragedy so He can use them strategically.

God often places local churches and loving people in the midst of tragedy so He can use them strategically. A friend of mine, Fernando, planted Mile High Calvary in Highlands Ranch, Colorado, about a month before we started Awaken. About nine years into the church, he started a Biblical Counseling school at their church. As the first round of thirty trained counselors drew close to graduation, they were wondering how they would keep thirty new counselors busy. Then came May 7, 2019. Just eight miles from where the shooting at Columbine High School had taken place over twenty years prior, another school shooting happened at the S.T.E.M. School. That school was directly across the street from Mile High Calvary, where the church had relocated to just a few years prior. Calvary became the natural shelter and connection place for families and First Responders. Life Flight helicopters landed in their church parking lot and the church doors flew open as a place of literal and spiritual shelter for families in a time of chaos and fear. Not only could they provide shelter, but they could provide more Biblical counseling than almost any church anywhere. They had a team of thirty trained Biblical counselors chomping at the bit, ready to go! The church's placement and the timing of their Biblical counseling school was no accident; it was strategic. God knew what He was doing. In that case, maybe S.T.E.M. didn't stand for Science, Technology, Engineering, and Mathematics as much as it stood for Strategically Timed Eternal Ministry.

God strategically placed Calvary across the street from where the shooting would take place and He strategically placed Awaken Church in Riverside Center where the flood would take place. And if you will follow His lead, He will do the same with you.

One of God's favorite pseudonyms to work under is "coincidence." As the Alpha and Omega, the Beginning and the End, the God who was and is and is to come, He sees it all. He has a way of strategically placing us where He needs us and where He can use us the greatest.

Be forewarned: often times, His placement comes at great personal cost to you. Don't view it as a cost though; view it as an eternal investment. The return on investment is huge and eternal!

CONDUITS OF COMFORT

As I write this, I just got off the phone with a friend of mine who found out hours ago that his wife miscarried their six-week-old baby. Their hearts are crushed. They were so excited and had already shared the news with so many people. He even sent me a picture of their ultrasound, their tiny little baby surrounded by a sea of black and gray.

I wish I didn't know their pain.

Jenn gave birth to two healthy girls, Emery and Adalyn, then suddenly and unexpectedly, miscarried our next two. After two painful, surprising, crushing miscarriages, we were apprehensive about another pregnancy. Even when Jenn got pregnant again, we were hesitant to celebrate, not knowing if it would end again in heart-wrenching loss. Thankfully Jenn gave birth to a healthy baby boy, Haddon Graham. We have three kids on earth and we can't wait to meet Eden and Ellis one day in heaven!

When I talked with my friend on the phone today, I comforted him with the comfort I had received years ago. This is how God works. He uses our pain and loss to craft us into conduits of comfort in the lives of the people around us. I told him that although he didn't sign up for this, God was going to use it in his life. One day, I believe he and his wife will be on the other side of that phone call or sitting in a living room with someone who is struggling through that same pain. They will be able to relate and speak hope, just like Jenn and I can now.

> He uses our pain and loss to craft us into conduits of comfort in the lives of the people around us.

I didn't sign up for that pain. I didn't ask for it and I wasn't prepared for it. I don't want to relate to kids whose parents are divorced, parents who have miscarried, pastors who are struggling to provide for their families, or church planters who have lost virtually everything. God didn't want those for me either, but He can use them.

Pain and suffering were never part of God's original plan. After creating everything in Genesis 1, He stood back like an artist admiring His work and said it was "very good." He was proud. Death and loss were not in the picture. Then Satan rolled onto the scene... or should I say slithered into the scene, bringing death, loss, shame, and fear in his wake.

As the Redeemer, God is able to miraculously use for our good what the devil intended for evil. Miscarriages, financial loss, a medical diagnosis, and even a shooting and a flood... Although He didn't cause them, He will use them if we will trust Him.

MAKE IT RAIN

The week before the flood hit Clarksville, I had scheduled my first board meeting. I barely knew what to do in a board meeting, but I was the president of the board and we had a conference call scheduled for May 5. One of our agenda items was discussing me beginning to get my first paycheck from the church. Awaken was small, but slowly growing in numerical and financial strength and I was excited to be able to focus a little more on the church as soon as I could begin getting paid by the church. Our meeting was scheduled for May 5, but the flood hit May 3. Amidst the chaos, confusion, grieving, and loss of that week, I also mourned the loss of a paycheck. What may seem trivial was a huge loss for our family. Since the church had incurred such a huge financial blow due to the flood, I assumed me getting a paycheck was out of the question.

As the story of the flood quickly spread online, we got hit with another flood. But this time, it wasn't floodwaters, it was finances. Donations began pouring in from coast to coast, from New York to California and New Mexico to Montana, and around the world. The donations gave us more than enough money to rebuild and relaunch. We ended up being one of the first businesses on Riverside Drive to reopen and Nashville News Channel 7 came and did a story on us on our grand reopening morning. Thanks to generous donations from around the world, we emerged from the flood far stronger financially than we had been going into the flood! Not only was I still able to begin receiving pay from the church after the flood, due to the donations that came in, I was able to receive even more than the board had originally planned! Go ahead - tell God what you think is impossible or hopeless! He may just surprise you.

> **"When you go through deep waters, I will be with you. When you go through rivers of difficulty, you will not drown..."**
> **(Isaiah 43:2 NLT)**

Come hell or high water, He's got you.

The flood seemed to usher in a flood of growth, a season that lasted for the next few years. After the flood waters cleared out and we kicked through the walls, rebuilt, repainted, and relaunched...we outgrew our tiny 2,400 square feet in three months. Since the businesses around the shopping center had relocated after the flood, we were able to move into a former foster care building across the parking lot and renovate the space on the landlord's dime. He even let us choose the layout! God was still at work, redeeming the flood.

We chose the layout to fit our needs and moved in on Christmas Eve a couple months later. It wasn't long until we outgrew that space and began building out in the adjacent store front. From there, we would eventually add the next space over — a former Curves womens gym — and the storage space next to it, completing our takeover of the entire 9,600 square feet. We renovated the Curves space into a second venue, which would house another 110 seats and have a large wall-size HD video screen where people could view a livestream of the video teaching from the venue three doors down. It was a second venue...on the same campus. If that wasn't crazy enough, five years into our church, the entire shopping center went on the market and we were able to purchase the whole thing!

We now own the shopping center where we once lost everything!

What a wild ride!

I love telling that story because it reminds me of God's faithfulness. But just like you, my memory can be pretty faulty. At times, it's so much easier to remember hardships, failures, and hear the voice of the critics.

Over the years I've learned that our longevity in ministry depends on our commitment to fight forgetfulness. If you let it, the volume of your critics will overpower the displays of God's faithfulness throughout your life and ministry. Don't let the complainers turn into joy stealers or the hardships turn into miracle-killers. Remind the devil what Nehemiah reminded his opposition: "you have no portion or right or claim" (Nehemiah 2:20 ESV).

Our longevity in ministry depends on
our commitment to fight forgetfulness.

MONUMENTS DRIVE THE MOVEMENT

One of our core values at Awaken says, *"Monuments drive the movement. We intentionally take time to remember and celebrate God's faithfulness. Our past victories are vital for future success, and being used by God is a privilege and honor that we will never take for granted."* Our forward motion in ministry is fueled by the monuments we build along the way.

--- **99** ---

Our forward motion in ministry is
fueled by the monuments we build
along the way.

Building monuments was not just our idea, though. God and His people were big on monuments throughout the Old Testament. The early books of the Bible are filled with altars and monuments that were built as reminders of a time God showed up or something specific He spoke.

One of my favorite examples is when God led Israel through the flooding Jordan River in Joshua 3. It was nothing short of miraculous. Israel did their part and God did His part. Every single person and animal and all their possessions crossed through the river on dry ground. As if parting the river wasn't miraculous enough, God even dried up the riverbed so they wouldn't have to try to trudge through the muddy remains Spartan race style.

What they witnessed that day was nothing short of a miracle, and God wasn't about to let them forget it. As soon as the final people crossed over, God had one more set of directions for Joshua.

God told them, "...Take twelve stones from here out of the midst of the Jordan, from the very place where the priests' feet stood firmly, and bring them over with you and lay them down in the place where you lodge tonight" (Joshua 4:3 ESV).

What do you do when God tells you to pile up twelve river rocks? You pile up twelve river rocks. And don't just think of smooth stones you'd skip across a river. For this to be the eye-catching display God wanted it to be, these would have to be river boulders.

We're not done, though. Don't miss this last detail. It wasn't only the pile God was concerned with; the placement of the pile was important as well. God told them to carry the boulders and "lay them down in the place where you lodge tonight." As soon as they arrived at their lodging place, Gilgal, they assembled the monument.

The pile of boulders would remind the future generations of God's faithfulness, but the current generation needed reminding as well. Only a few days later, one of the most infamous marches would begin: the one-week march around Jericho. Every morning as the Israelite army left camp to march around Jericho, they saw that pile of river boulders. Last week, those boulders had been buried under the flooding Jordan River, but God performed the impossible. Imagine the faith that pile of stones must have roused in them each morning! And later that day, after they had marched around the whole city, maybe even with insults from the people of Jericho raining down on them, and again when they had noticed that after days of marching, the walls looked as impenetrable as ever, they went back to their camp at Gilgal. As they marched back into camp, that monument reminded them of God's miraculous intervention on their behalf.

Monuments build our faith and keep us moving, even when continuing to move forward seems like an exercise in futility.

Monuments come in all shapes and sizes, by the way. Here are a few examples of monuments we have built over the last decade at Awaken Church...

Photos

A giant pile of river boulders may not be the most welcoming sight in your church's entryway, but a nicely framed picture of that special scene may be. All around our church you'll find canvas pictures of monumental events: our first church service back in 2009, our flooded sanctuary from 2010, the first time we broke 1,000 people at Easter in 2012, our fifth birthday in 2014, and a picture of five of us praying for a building that is now our South Venue. Monuments are everywhere because temptations to quit and tendency to forget are everywhere.

Celebrations

We build monuments every time our church turns another year old. We celebrate the things God has done in the past year and look ahead to what we believe He's going to do. Balloons, cupcakes, baptisms, free espresso, confetti... you never know what will happen at an Awaken birthday party!

Email

In my email inbox, I have a folder called "monuments" where I file away positive, encouraging things people send me. Periodically, I'll scroll through and remember stories of how God has changed lives.

Artwork

I love the creative ideas our team comes up with at Awaken. When we built our cafe and collaborative meeting space, The Socialside, we designed it with a built-in monument, The Floodline. We have a white line that cuts through the red walls all the way around the room that reminds us of how deep the water once was in that very building. Interestingly, two days before we opened The Socialside, I called an emergency meeting with our staff to share some tough struggles we were facing. That Floodline immediately went to work on our behalf. As I shared some seemingly impossible barriers we were up against, I pointed to the Floodline and reminded them, "If God could take us through the flood, He can take us through this, too."

Not only does the Floodline work in that way, but our Creative Team was even able to track down some driftwood from the 2010 flood. They cut it up, mounted it to the wall, and included it as part of the decor when we opened a new Kindergarten room. The wood that used to be floating through our parking lot is now a display of art on our wall!

In the Reach room of The Socialside, you'll find a wallsize hand-painted map with little red pins spread all over the map. Each pin represents one of the eighty-eight countries (so far) that have tuned into our livestream over the years.

Websites

Our "Ministries We Support" page serves not only as information about our ministry partners, but also as a running tally of how many hundreds of thousands of dollars (eventually millions) we have given to them over the years! We partner with ministries, both locally and globally that enable us to reach people with the hope of the Gospel. The web page reminds us of how we are empowering the Gospel to get into the hearts of hungry homeless people, hurting single mothers, kids in after school Bible programs, and even tribes who had previously never heard the Bible in their own native language!

So what has God done in and through you or your church? And more importantly, how you can make sure you never forget it?

Whether your floodwaters are literal or physical, you'll face them along with people throwing fits and your own temptation to want to quit. We have dealt with all of the above and I know more challenges lie ahead. With the guaranteed forecast of storms ahead, you'll need a strategy for when they come.

SEVEN

SPOT LIGHTS AND STAB WOUNDS

Leading can be lonely and painful.

I read a tweet recently from a well-known, world-touring, Christian conference speaker about her resilience in ministry. She said the thought of quitting has never entered her mind, not even for a second.

Sounds amazing, right? What an inspiration!

Here's my problem: I can't relate to it. I really want to connect with that sentiment of never wanting to quit. I really wish I could honestly say something like that and mean it. I wish that "not for a second" did I want to end my race early because it just feels too exhausting to move forward. I wish I didn't feel depressed at times like Elijah did or question my calling like Moses.

Unfortunately, I can only partially relate to her sentiment.

She mentioned that what keeps her going is that she is in it for Jesus, who keeps her and sustains her. I can relate to that part. Not only can I relate, but I fully agree. I also agree with being in ministry for Jesus and I too recognize He is my keeper, sustainer, and all of my reasons to persevere.

The part I struggled with was not wanting to quit early. Although I know one day I will cross the finish line, I would be lying if I said I didn't, at times, feel ready to stop and drop now, or even on a Sunday morning.

My version of that tweet would sound much different because sometimes the finish line seems way too far in the distance and a different lifestyle and career path seem a lot easier. Ten years in, you wouldn't think that would still be the case, right? After all, I'm the pastor. Pastors aren't *supposed* to feel that way. Pastors are *supposed* to be fired up in prayer, fueled up with caffeine, and forging forward in faith.

Says who? Who made that rule?

I am that way usually, but not always. There have been times when I didn't want to get out of bed on a Sunday morning, but I did because everyone was expecting me to show up and preach at all of our services that day. One Sunday in particular, I pushed through the first two services, then holed up in my office afterward, wanting so badly to leave as the third service started. I asked Jenn to pray for me before I walked in to preach then wiped the tears back and went up anyway. As I started into the message, I felt so fake. So I stopped. Inexplicably, I didn't feel like I could keep going. Before I realized what was happening, the pastors were on the stage with me, hands on me, praying for me as I sobbed. That's not normally how I feel, but it has happened.

Not only have I struggled with those feelings, but I also have a tendency to isolate. I would describe myself as a high-functioning introvert that often has to function as an extrovert. I'm naturally an introvert, as are a surprising amount of pastors, but my role as a leader of people forces me to be an extrovert. Don't get me wrong, I enjoy being with people and for the most part I'm good with people, but like my wife enjoys her coffee with plenty of half and half, I prefer my extroversion with plenty of time to myself and my family. Those are the cream and sugar that make life sweet.

And while I'm on the topic of my wife, sometimes she wants to quit too. I know, I know. She's not *supposed* to feel that way either. She's *supposed* to be always smiling, perpetually ready to pray for people, and hospitable to the most grouchy, selfish people who give her unwanted fashion advice and vocalize their negative opinion of her nose ring and tattoo (and if I have it my way, tattoos). According to most stereotypes, "God bless you" and "How can I help?" should be the first words out of her mouth constantly, right along with a word of encouragement and a Crock-Pot full of food for the latest hurting family. Jenn is the most merciful, discerning, Jesus-loving person I know, but she's also not your stereotypical "pastor's wife." Along with her piercings and tattoo, she also has deep scars from her past, the pain of two miscarriages, betrayal from people we trusted, and a heart that is so loving that she often carries weight she isn't meant to carry.

Part of our strategy in not quitting is hoping we don't want to quit at the same time! And so far, except for a couple rare exceptions, that's always been the case. We cheer each other on when the other one has no cheering left in them.

And while we're at it with the secrets, here's one more: we're both seeing counselors.

Gasp!

If we haven't shattered your stereotypes and expectations already, the counselor mention may have done it. Some of you want to put the book down after reading that.

"Isn't the Holy Spirit enough? His name is 'Counselor' after all."

"What happened to having faith in God?"

"Maybe they should pray more."

All of us should probably pray more. You included. Am I right?

Like your mom told you about broccoli when you were a kid, don't knock it till you try it. Counseling has been life-changing for me and I would recommend it for everyone, whether you feel messed up or not. In fact, if we would let pastors be real people, we would have fewer pastors balancing on pedestals and plunging into moral failure. Scandalous sin is the result of the inability or unwillingness to be real. Some pastors choose not to be real, others feel they can't be. I refuse to be either.

Counseling has been life-changing for me and I would recommend it for everyone, whether you feel messed up or not.

So why the heavy hearts, you ask? Why does the burden seem so heavy at times? Why isn't ministry all prayer times and encouragement and miracles and smiles and happiness?

The short answer is the devil is real, life is painful, and our world is broken.

The devil is real, life is painful, and our world is broken.

The longer answer is the rest of this chapter. I am not writing this chapter in order to be depressing and I've been careful with the stories I'm sharing, in order to protect the guilty. This book and this chapter in particular are not written as a venting session or to be a cheap jab at people who have jabbed and stabbed me. I just want to give an honest peek at the unique challenges of leadership in the church. Whether you are a church planter not fully aware of what lies ahead, a pastor that relates to a lot of this, or a Christian looking for a unique vantage point, these stories will help you.

Buckle up and journey with me as I describe firsthand some of the challenges we have faced and how we have learned to stop at nothing to keep going and keep growing.

YOU WON'T KNOW UNTIL YOU KNOW

I had been told leadership is lonely, but I was the youth pastor. How could I understand what I was walking into as a church planter and lead pastor? The youth pastor doesn't make the final decisions and he doesn't feel the weight of the Lead Pastor. The youth pastor's job is to act like an adult when the parents are around and like a middle schooler when they're not. Sometimes we went a little too far and new rules were put in place because of us.

"Do not use condiments for games on the grass" or "Do not use church vehicles to ghost ride the whip" or "no more purchasing live goldfish" are actual rules that were put in place because of things I did. Depending on who's asking, I may or may not be proud of those moments and there may or may not be video proof that they happened.

Being a youth pastor is excellent preparation for pastoring a church — arguably the best — but it's still not the same thing. I can tell you all day what it's like to be six feet five inches tall, but you will never really know until you have walked a day in my size thirteen shoes and walked into a chandelier that almost required stitches (yes, that really happened).

Being on a church staff certainly does pull back the curtain on ministry and church leadership unlike when you are just attending a church. However, a peek behind the curtain isn't the same as working and living behind said curtain.

During my time on staff at our church in New Mexico, I was included in plenty of discussions and meetings that were a bit above my paygrade. I realize now they were training me by simply allowing me to listen. There were also plenty of meetings I was purposely kept out of (probably plenty I will never even know about). In hindsight, my pastor did a phenomenal job of training me without jading me. Some of the meetings too soon would have been too much.

All of that to say this: there are some things you will never be fully prepared for until you walk into them and are forced to deal with them.

99

There are some things you will never be fully prepared for until you walk into them and are forced to deal with them.

That is certainly the case with loneliness in leadership. Brace yourself for it, but just come to terms with the fact that you can't fully understand until you've lived it. I can tell you the stab wounds from a friend are painful, deep, and often heal slowly, but you won't know till you get stabbed. I'm not trying to be dramatic; I'm just saying that leadership is lonely...and sometimes a bit bloody.

I know I'm not painting a very pretty picture of church planting or pastoring. "Bloody" isn't a word that's going to send people lining up to plant churches. But I didn't write this book to win you over to church planting or ministry; I'm trying to prep you in a way that I wasn't. If you are called to this and driven by the Spirit, what I'm sharing with you can't possibly scare you out of it. In fact, I may be amping you up even further, like a cowboy getting ready to get on the back of an angry, 2,000-pound bull. Now that I think about it, the pain, adrenaline, exhaustion, and unknowns of bull riding are a pretty accurate illustration of church planting. I would know. I've done both.

LONELY LEADERS

My mom moved to Clarksville about a year into our church plant. I'm so glad she's part of our lives and our church. Recently, she met a young, college-aged guy who has been coming to Awaken for about a year and introduced herself. She said, "Hi! I'm Debbie. I'm Kevin's mom." He thought for a minute, then he said, "Kevin... Hmmm... I'm sure I'd know him if I saw him." She said, "Yeah, you probably would. He's the pastor." Red faced, he admitted he did in fact know who Kevin is! Most people do, obviously. When I meet visitors at our church, one of the first things they often tell me is that they have been on our website watching my messages. By default, I'm the the main face and voice of Awaken.

Standing in front of people every weekend can give people the false notion that they know you when they actually only know *about* you. There's a big difference between knowing *about* someone and actually *knowing* them. I know a lot about a bunch of old dead preachers (D.L. Moody is one of my favorites), but I obviously don't know them. Fact: I know Dwight K. Schrute farms beets, likes *Battlestar Galactica,* and can raise and lower his cholesterol at will, but I don't really know him.

This may surprise you, but Jenn and I don't get nearly as many invitations to parties and hang outs as many people assume we do. The introvert side of me is A-OK with that, but sometimes it does get old feeling like we are normally the initiators. In the rare times when someone invites us somewhere, Jenn or I sometimes jokingly exclaim, "We do have friends!"

I'm not writing this to get your pity; I'm writing this to pull back the curtain on reality. Although your reality will differ from ours, there will be plenty of overlap. One pastor's wife we talked to recently on this subject said, "I came to realize that I can't be real close friends with the other pastors' wives. I had to be ok with the fact that most of my closest friends live out of state." That was shocking to hear because we assumed it was much different, especially for her, a well-known speaker and author. Surely she has plenty of close friends nearby...right?

Leading a small group, attending parties, and even being in meetings are different when you're the lead pastor. And when you're at a meal with another family or a group, you'd better be ready to pray because you'll definitely be asked. "Pastor, will you pray for us?"

One of the weirdest things about being a pastor is when you meet strangers. Sometimes I try to dodge the subject of careers or at least what I do for a living because the moment I say, "I'm a pastor..." it's like everything goes into slow motion. The person immediately begins thinking back through the conversation, trying to remember which four-letter words they used. They feel prompted to tell you when the last time they want to church was and they start using words they never use, like "parishioners" and "clergy."

Even leading a small group is different for Jenn and me.

We want to be real and raw, but some information is just too much information for the pastor to share with a group of people new to the church.

Now that our kids are getting older, one of the most challenging parts of people getting mad and leaving is that sometimes, they take our kids' friends with them. I can let things roll off my back, but it's hard to watch when my kids get hurt and don't understand.

Leadership is lonely. A lot of people know your name, but very few people actually know you.

99

Leadership is lonely. A lot of people know your name, but very few people actually know you.

SITCOMS, PHARISEES, AND THE SECOND COMING

Criticism will come from every angle, often when you least expect it. One of the most jarring criticisms I received early on came when we were just getting started. The church was only a month or two old and I remember seeing a new guy walk in. When your church has twenty adults, the new guy stands out! Since he walked in right as we started, I didn't get to talk with him, but he stayed through the whole service, then sneaked out the door right as we were ending. I figured I had missed my chance to talk with him. Little did I know, I'd have a surprise waiting in my inbox shortly. I don't have the email anymore (I probably tried to erase it from my memory), but I can vividly remember some of his critique. According to his wildly flattering critique, I was "a chore to listen to," "taught for far too long," and I needed to be more "relevant to the culture." He went on to give his two cents (actually, if we're going by word count, it was probably more like $2.25) about how adult attention spans happen in twenty-three-minute sitcom increments and how I had no right to "impose church culture on a culture I clearly didn't understand."

I was shaken up by that email, so I sent it to my pastor to get some feedback. This is part of my pastor's actual email response to me:

"Having this guy come in and tell you this is EXCELLENT! Couldn't happen at a better time. It helps to crystalize who YOU are and the difference between emergent (Biblical-authority-doubting) and your ministry."

"EXCELLENT"?! Not only is that not the word I would use to describe that email, but "excellent" was in ALL CAPS?! He went on to encourage me to stay true to God's Word and not be swayed by the critics. In response to my critic, he also said,

"Since when is truth irrelevant? Should Paul have spent more time teaching the Corinthians about Greco-Roman musical trends? Should his message to the believers at Troas have been cut short (he preached 'til after midnight)? This is all good for you to know who you are and know your ministry. Don't change a thing!!!!!!"

Let me restate that gold nugget of truth he just dropped, in case you missed it: "This is all good for you to know who you are and know your ministry."

Translation: critics, whether they're trying to help or trying to hurt (you will encounter both, but they will often sound very similar), can really only help you grow.

Critics, whether they're trying to help or
trying to hurt (you will encounter both,
but they will often sound very similar),
can really only help you grow.

Reread that last sentence and let it sink in. They may be out to sabotage you, but they're actually pouring Miracle-Gro on you.

Regardless of what they say or how they say it, you have the opportunity to grow in how you respond to them and what you do with what they say. Hint: if you change the way you lead every time someone disagrees, you should go ahead and update your résumé. You won't be leading much longer.

I've been accused of lots of things, called names, and had

my character and priorities questioned and attacked a lot in the last decade. Pharisee, apostate, and "unbiblical" stand out among the names people have used to describe me, among other things. I've been accused of being too structured, not structured enough, untouchable, unapproachable, uncaring, and dismissive. Some say I'm too harsh, others say I'm too lenient. One friend of mine abruptly ended our relationship via email after I called him out on an issue I saw. We even had some of our closest friends distance themselves from us until I found out from another pastor they were attending his church! That one stung and took some time to heal.

We've escorted people off of our property and called the Police on a protester who insisted that Jesus was coming back on September 23 (it was awkward running into him later on in October, post-Second Coming!). One lady even tried to run one of our pastors over with her truck in the parking lot! He dodged it and is ready once she gets out of jail, in case she violates her restraining order.

STONED AND SNAKEBITTEN

One of the first major head-on opinion collisions we had with someone was with a family who had been with us from the very beginning. We had a disagreement over a ministry they wanted to start but I didn't feel we were ready for yet. After months of sit-down conversations, we still couldn't come to an agreement. Things finally came to a head, and I had a very clear "cease and desist" chat with her and her husband—and cease they did. They ceased attending our church, went to another local church, and dragged a dozen or so families with them.

That Sunday as they joined us for their final time, I continued teaching through the next passage in the book of Joshua which happened to be about unity in the church. "God is glorified when His people are unified," I said, and with that, they vacated and divided.

The flood was a tough storm to weather, but this felt even harder.

As long and drawn out and painful as that ordeal was for Jenn and I and our team, we would quickly learn that it was just the beginning. Throughout the years, many people have drawn lines in the sand, choosing to die on hills not worthy of dying on. In addition, we would also learn that having people leave can be a really good thing. For us, it was healthy for the division and its leaders to get out of the church. For those who left, it was healthy for them to be part of a church elsewhere that was healthy and running fine long before they showed up.

Sometimes it's healthy to remember we are all replaceable.

Sometimes it's healthy to remember
we are all replaceable.

Unfortunately, division in the church always causes collateral damage. Many of the families who got caught up in the drama and dragged with them ended up falling away from church altogether.

The following is a list of actual reasons people have given for leaving our church over the years (many are not listed):

"The music is too loud."

"You don't go to lunch with me anymore."

"You don't teach like you used to."

"You talk about money way too much."

"The church is getting too big and you're unapproachable."

"Jesus wouldn't have been as harsh with His disciples as you are with me."

"We're just not being fed anymore."

"The music you play here isn't holy."

I sat down with a new family once after I finished preaching and they told me about their one to ten rating scale they used to rate sermons. I didn't ask what my sermon ranked that day. I also didn't share what I would have ranked them.

I've learned that when someone shows up at our church

bad mouthing his last pastor or church in an attempt to build me or our church up, I had better send them packing or nip that in the bud real quick. It won't take long until I inevitably say or do something they don't like and they pack their bags and bad mouth me at their next spiritual pit stop.

The crazy thing is when I go from one person who is so thankful for the message to a critic in the very next conversation! This is nothing new though. People have been fickle since the beginning of time.

In Acts 14, Paul and Barnabas were hailed as gods after healing a guy in the city of Lystra. In the very next paragraph, some of the people of Lystra stone Paul and leave him for dead. In Acts 28, the people on the island of Malta thought Paul was receiving justice when a snake jumped out of the campfire and bit him. However, after he shook off the snake and didn't fall over dead, they worshiped him as a god. From demonized to worshiped within just a few hours! People's opinions change daily, hourly and sometimes even from conversation to conversation. You can't base your ministry on what people say today. It will be different on Tuesday.

CHURCH HOPPERS

Serial church hopping is a plague in Christianity today. This is not how God intended His church to function. After hopping in and out of multiple churches for years, sometimes going, sometimes not, and never really committing themselves anywhere, it's funny to me that some people seem surprised at the lack of spiritual growth in their lives. I'm also saddened for those who don't even realize their lack of growth. It's no wonder. If you transplant a tree every few years, never allowing its roots to grow deep and thick, that tree definitely will not thrive and it may not even live very long.

The list of reasons to stay rooted in a local church is far longer than the very small list of reasons to leave.

Part of stopping at nothing to build the church is regularly reminding those under our care that the list of reasons to stay rooted in a local church is far longer than the very small list of reasons to leave. Paul described the church as "the household of God" in his first letter to Timothy. We are part of the same household! If you are a follower of Jesus, the same blood that bought me bought you! Families don't give up on each other. Your church needs you and you need your church.

The only Biblical reasons I know of to leave a church are as follows:

Unrepentant sin on behalf of the leadership (1 Timothy 5:19 ESV). If a leader is living in sin and is unwilling to repent, it may be time to go. Stay approachable and accountable so as to avoid appearances of evil and causing people to stumble. Flaunting a liberty you have could inadvertently give someone an excuse to leave.

False teaching or unresolvable theological issues (2 Peter 2:1-3 ESV, Jude 4 ESV). If false teaching is worthy of God's judgment as those passages state, it is something worth dividing over. I've had hard conversations with people who had fundamentally different theological beliefs and we realized departure may be the only answer. Although changing their theology would be ideal, their stubbornness and theological error can quickly become poison in your church.

A change of season (Acts 13:1-3 ESV). If their job is moving them to a new city, their commute has changed and they are living in a different community, or the Lord is specifically leading them elsewhere, it may be time for them to move on. In those cases, help them transition well. Help them find a church or connect them to community when you are able. Not only are you promoting their spiritual growth, but you're leaving the door open if they ever return.

"Church hopping" is a phenomena in modern Christianity which was not possible in the early New Testament church. In the early days, leaving your local church and going down the street or a few blocks away where the music was better and the kids ministry had nicer play equipment was unheard of.

Picky, selfish reasons are not a reason for people to leave; in fact, they are more so a reason to stay and work things out. This is what we do as Christians. Paul tells us in Ephesians 4 ESV to "bear with one another." He's saying that we love each other even when we don't like each other. Ministry affords us many opportunities to live this out by loving difficult people.

I've found that most people who leave for unbiblical reasons tend to justify their actions by demonizing their leaders, exaggerating the problems, and causing division. If they can stir the pot a little, it may make them feel more justified in their decision to hop on over to the next place.

If you are a church hopper or you know one, remember: there is no such thing as a perfect church. And if by chance you find a perfect church, get out of there before you ruin it!

BEWARE OF THE CAVE PEOPLE

"If you're a Christian who is sitting in a chair every Sunday, not giving, and not serving, you're taking up a seat for someone who needs to hear about Jesus."

99

There is no such thing as a perfect church. And if by chance you find a perfect church, get out of there before you ruin it!

I've told that to our church a few times and I don't plan on stopping. Some people are thankful for my honesty and I have heard others are not. It's genuinely how I feel, though. I'm pro-participation and I'm pretty sure the Holy Spirit is, too. Check 1 Corinthians 12-14 and let me know if you read it differently.

My goal in telling people that was not to clear the chairs, but to capture attention and call the church to action. To the guy with folded arms, waiting on our team to entertain him and watch his kids: do you know how Google works? Just search "churches in Clarksville" and you'll get hundreds of results. I guarantee you'll find a few churches who will bend over backwards to keep your butt planted in one of their chairs week after week. It won't be Awaken Church though. People are dying and need to hear the Gospel. There's urgency in our mission. If you're looking for a show on Sundays, the movie theaters and mall are open and will gladly accept the money you refuse to give to the church.

There's no more guaranteed way to burn out in ministry than to try to make everyone happy. Twister is a fun game when you're thirteen and still flexible, but it's not fun when you're trying to lead while keeping your head above the flood of unsolicited opinions.

Every church has C.A.V.E. people. C.A.V.E. people are Completely Against Virtually Everything and it's a waste of time to try to engage them and argue with them. Paul told Timothy to stay away from "irreverent, silly" arguments (1 Timothy 4:7 ESV) and instead, train for godliness.

This is a vital truth to remember, but an easy one to forget—especially when you're dodging flaming arrows coming not from the outside world but from the seats in front of you. This truth is so important that we included it as one of twelve parts of our Awaken Church Code. We say it this way:

"We can't please everybody. We encourage input, but our main objective is reaching people with the Gospel. We unite behind the pastoral vision, structure, and leadership set forth by God's Word, regardless of negative criticism."

It may sound negative, but it's not. It keeps us focused on our main objective instead of arguing about rabbit trails and self-centered opinions.

This is also where our vision statement comes in handy:

"Awakening people far from Christ to new life in Christ."

I didn't move 1,200 miles to grow the church by transplanting picky Christians from other local churches. Please, please stay where you are! We want to populate heaven and depopulate hell by reaching people who are far from Christ.

We want to populate heaven and depopulate hell by reaching people who are far from Christ.

If Jesus' mission was to seek and save the lost, we will adopt that as our mission as well. *Until everyone knows Jesus or we die trying!*

DON'T MEET WITH SANBALLAT

Not everything is worth going to battle over or even having a meeting over. There are some, but learn to be selective. Make sure the hill you choose is one worth dying on and refuse to take every meeting people want to air their grievances. You have ground to take for the gospel. In the words of Nehemiah to his opposition, Sanballat and Tobiah: "...I am doing a great work and I cannot come down. Why should the work stop while I leave it and come down to you" (Nehemiah 6:3 ESV).

Nehemiah was onto something there. When you take time to sit down with someone and let them air their opinions about things that don't matter to the overall vision, you have to hit pause on the work. The hour you spent with them was an hour you could have spent pouring into someone who is helping move the vision forward. Most battles aren't worth fighting and many aren't even worth having a meeting about. We have people to reach. Either join us or don't, but please don't distract us.

You'll have to be careful with how you say that, though. Anyone who knows who Sanballat and Tobiah are won't like being compared to them.

Paul said, "Speak the truth in love." The way you say something is as or more important as what you actually say. Am I right, parents? When your kid says, "Sorry!" with a snotty, snappy attitude, their words don't match up with the vibe they're giving out. Gentleness is not a specialty of mine, so I've had to work hard on this and apologize about this over the years. Keep working on gentleness. Being firm with someone doesn't necessarily mean you're not being loving.

Sometimes it helps me to write out some of the things I'm going to say as I prepare to walk into a challenging meeting or conversation. One time, I wrote an email to a guy who had recently left our church, letting him know what I thought about his immature decision. Thankfully I let my wife read the email before I sent it. She recommended I send it to a gentle, wise, unbiased friend of mine to have him look over it. He ended up putting it into a Google Doc and suggesting edits on about seventy-five percent of it. When I read the final draft to Jenn, she asked how much of it I had actually written! Had I hit "send" on that first draft, my hurt and harsh tone probably would have done more harm than help. If you struggle with gentleness like I do, surround yourself with gentle people and learn from them.

And by the way, when people leave, let them leave. You may be tempted to try to chase every person down who leaves your team or your church. You can't possibly put out every fire, so save your energy for the ones you should chase down. I've found that it's healthier for us and sometimes for others when they leave and go bloom somewhere else. Embrace that and find the freedom that comes with it! And thank God for the times when they choose to leave on their own.

You have probably gone to a restaurant or a store and thought, "I could run this place much better," or "I would do things much differently." If you're a leader, I guarantee you have. Sometimes it's hard not to. Here's the hard reality about your leadership: many people would lead differently if they were in charge. That's ok.

Except for a few examples of people falling into sin or developing big theological differences, many people have left our church throughout the years because if they were the lead pastor, they would lead our church differently than I do. The feelings are mutual. If they were leading it, I'd do it differently, too. That's ok. Different isn't always right or wrong, it's just different. Although in most cases, I don't think that's a valid reason to leave, try to boil the problem down to the main issue. I've found this to be the most common one. Ninety percent of the picky opinions translate to "If I were in charge, I'd do it differently." If they can't change their mind and follow your lead, it might be healthy for them to go somewhere where they can receive leadership from the pastor. Open the door, give them an off ramp and your blessing, pray for them, and let them go. You'll both be better for it. Critics are everywhere. People will come and go. As long as you walk in integrity as the leader God has called you to be, keep your head up, eyes on Jesus, and follow Him no matter who goes with you.

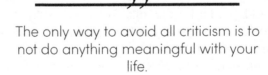

The only way to avoid all criticism is to not do anything meaningful with your life.

THAT CRITICISM TO WORK!

Critics are to leaders what mosquitoes are to a hot, humid Tennessee summer. Sometimes they appear in droves and can make life miserable. You were just minding your own business, and suddenly here they come, cramping your style. Although no one likes criticism, it's part of leadership. The only way to avoid all criticism is to not do anything meaningful with your life. If you plan to live for something important, expect critics. As Victor Hugo once quipped, "You have enemies? Why, it is the story of every man who has done a great deed or created a new idea."

Through the criticism I've received over the years, I've learned some helpful things to do with it.

Be encouraged by it. The only people who get criticized are the people who are doing something. It's a lot easier to do nothing and criticize those who are than go out and put work in. So when you are criticized, before you receive it as a punch in the face, let it first be a pat on the back. Good work for going out and doing some work!

I know criticism is rarely encouraging, but not only is it a reminder that you're doing something, it's also an opportunity to grow.

Listen to it. When criticism comes, the natural thing to do is go on the defense. While they are telling you what they think you've done wrong, you're already formulating your response and building your defense. Here's the better thing to do: listen.

They're probably expecting you to be defensive. If you can resist the urge to argue and choose to listen instead, you'll have their attention and help to disarm a potentially hostile situation.

Like the gum inside a Blow Pop, there's a lesson packaged inside that ball of criticism. Don't rob yourself of something you may need to learn simply because you don't want to learn it from the person delivering it. Let them deliver the message, then figure out what you're going to do with it.

Not only will changing your response to criticism help you, it may help your critic too. A person who came in to tell you how poor you are at leading may get a lesson in leadership from you as you sit and patiently listen. Even if the conversation doesn't end with you both agreeing on the topic, hopefully you can agree to disagree and demonstrate that you can disagree without being disagreeable. Not only that, but patient listening opens the door for you to speak truth into their life when the tables inevitably turn.

99

You can agree to disagree and
demonstrate that you can disagree
without being disagreeable.

Filter it. Coffee, water, and air all need to be filtered, and so does criticism. A mentor of ours gave Jenn and I this helpful three-part filter for criticism:

1) God: Pray about it first. Ask God to point out any areas of truth or anything He may be trying to point out to you (even if the messenger has plenty of their own flaws!). And while you're praying about that person's criticism, pray for the person. Jesus said to pray for our enemies and for those who persecute you. There's no better time than the present!

2) Spouse: Ask your spouse (or, if you're not married, the person who knows you best) if there's truth to anything that was said. This opens the door to helpful truth from someone who knows you well. It may be something they've wanted to bring up, but didn't know how to approach it. You opening the door for their perspective also opens the door for your personal growth.

3) Trusted friends: This assumes you are surrounded by some people who love you and speak truth into your life. If you're not, make that top priority. You won't last long without them. Ask them if there's truth to what was said, and if so, what to do about it. The same truth applies with this group: your openness is a leadership lesson to them and opens you to new opportunities for growth.

Learn from it. I know, I know. You wish the final step was "Shred it" or "Let them have it," or "Pull a Nehemiah 13 and rip their beards out," but it's not. There certainly is a time and place for ignoring criticism. For instance, when people leave snarky anonymous comments on giving envelopes or pieces of paper they drop into our giving boxes, I have a special procedure for those. We file those anonymous complaints in shiny, metal, cylindrical files placed conveniently around our campus.

Like it or not, we all have plenty of areas to grow, and

sometimes our weaknesses are highlighted in painful ways by negative people. Generally speaking, people are not out to hurt you, but even if they are, you can still learn from them. In fact, I've learned that the people who may be out to hurt you are often some of the most honest people because they don't care about your feelings. I know that's not comforting, but it's reality.

> Like it or not, we all have plenty of
> areas to grow, and sometimes our
> weaknesses are highlighted in painful
> ways by negative people.

Whether or not you learn from their actual words, you can always learn from the confrontation itself. Embrace it as part of life and ministry, learn and implement what you can, own and repent of any failures, then move forward. Thankfully God specializes in using flawed people like us!

LETHAL LIONS

I read a news story [1] recently about a lioness, Zuri, in an Indiana zoo who attacked and killed a male lion, Nyack, who was the father of their three cubs. Thankfully it happened before the zoo was open to the public, so five-year olds wouldn't be scarred when they watch *The Lion King* in the future. The lioness attacked the lion, pinned him down by the throat until he suffocated, while the zoo staff tried to separate them to no avail. One of the lion experts analyzing the rare event said, "When lions usually go after each other, they are happy to just wound each other." He went onto say, "All of these animals are unpredictable moment to moment. The main lesson here is... that it's something that can happen. If you have that combination of an aggressive female and submissive male, it might not be the ideal configuration."[1]

Lions are social animals, so each zoo typically owns a small pride of lions that they keep on display at different times. No matter how well the keepers know the lions or how well-behaved they tend to be, the reality is, they're still unpredictable wild animals and there's always a risk when they're living in the same confined space. Case in point, Zuri and Nyack (R.I.P.).

Like Zuri and Nyack, loneliness and criticism often dwell in close quarters in the lives of church leaders. And in the words of the lion expert, that's "not the ideal configuration." Since there's no way to eliminate them, it's important to know the hazards and potential dangers associated with them so you can be proactive. They can both be dangerous on their own, but unfortunately, like two aggressive lions confined in close quarters, loneliness can agitate your response to criticism and criticism can magnify and increase your loneliness. When they go at each other, the results can be devastating. Depression, panic attacks, suicide, alcoholism, and so much more are problems not only for those who sit in the church chairs, but also for many who stand on a stage behind a pulpit.

Let's fight this together. You may feel alone, but you're not actually alone. So much of my heart behind this book is talking about things that are ugly and painful with the hope that it spurs on conversation and initiates deeper relationships, preventing the lethal combination of loneliness and criticism. They're both dangerous in their own rite, but if approached correctly, they can be harnessed and used to promote growth and life!

PART THREE

UNTIL EVERYONE KNOWS

JESUS OR WE DIE TRYING

EIGHT

THREE WORDS THAT WILL CHANGE YOUR LIFE

Finding God's will isn't the issue; living in it is.

"I am pregnant."

Those three words changed my life, beginning one of the most amazing experiences of my life, raising little screaming, crying, puking, expensive, exhausting, exhilarating little humans.

"Out of coffee."

Those three words can also be life-changing, or at least day-changing.

"No waffle fries" were the three words the Chick-Fil-A employee muttered sheepishly, causing me to instinctively jump over the counter, pushing employees out of the way, spilling delicious lemonade all over the red tiled floor in search of the glorious, golden potatoes. Ok, I didn't actually jump the counter, but one of our local Chick-Fil-A locations did recently tell me that. That location will remain unnamed so as not to prevent future business.

Those are three examples of three-word phrases that will change your life or impact you greatly in some way. This chapter is not about any of those. I have three other words in mind.

Let's start with a backstory.

So much in life is a mystery. Throughout the years of the church, we've had a few mysteries to solve.

One Sunday morning, we discovered that a lady, probably high on something, broke into the business next door, Curves, a female-only workout studio. After breaking into Curves, the higher-than-a-kite burglar kicked holes through walls until she got into our building, a couple doors over. Thankfully all was intact besides

135

some gaping holes that we temporarily covered with cabinets so the babies couldn't crawl out and exercise at Curves.

Another time, a staff member's car was broken into behind our building. The fun part was watching it all unfold on our surveillance camera later on, notifying the police, and finding out the hoodlum was arrested during math class at his high school. I was always scared enough when I got called out of class to talk to the principal. I can only imagine early dismissal for a Police interrogation! The big blue truck he drove and the fact that he walked up to the camera, looked straight into it, then took a few minutes to hit the camera with a shoe, made him pretty easy to identify.

These days, when we're not forced to solve a mystery, we often pay to solve one. Murder mysteries, jewelry heists, escape games, and other real-life Clue games are all the rage.

Unfortunately, not all mysteries at our church, or in our lives or ministry, are easy to solve.

Although planting a church can feel a bit like an escape game (or at times, a why-did-they-stab-me-in-the-back-this-time mystery), and although it is often a step of faith into the dark, following God was never meant to be a scavenger hunt! God never intended us to be on a quest to "find God's will" as though if we harness our inner Nicholas Cage, skillfully figure out how to piece together the right clues, and unlock a hidden door with the decoder ring, we'll find it.

As we discussed in chapter one, I believe in a "calling" that God has on each person's life. I don't believe that God has put us in one end of a rat maze and our calling is the piece of cheese at the end. He's not a scientist studying how quickly and strategically we will find it and He's not receiving some sort of twisted pleasure by watching us make wrong turns and miss clues along the way.

Why have we reduced the beautiful, eternal, God-glorifying will of God into a scavenger hunt?

I'm sure there's some of this we've done unintentionally, but if we're honest, I think some of it is intentional. There is some pride at the root of this scavenger hunt. It appeals to our "conqueror" nature, especially found in men. Not only do we sometimes enjoy the struggle and intrigue of the journey, but we feel like we've arrived - like we've conquered - when we "figure it out."

That begins another set of necessary questions. Do we ever

really "figure it out"? And if we do, what then? Have we arrived? Is our calling complete? Is that when retirement starts?

Here's a crazy thought: what if it was never about conquering something or arriving safely on the other side? What if "success" was simply about being faithful and full of faith in the middle, in the dark, during the journey when a lot of it didn't seem to make sense?

99

What if "success" was simply about being faithful and full of faith in the middle, in the dark, during the journey when a lot of it didn't seem to make sense?

SPILLING COFFEE AND DRINKING COFFEE

About five years into Awaken, I met a guy on a Sunday morning at church right after he had spilled coffee all over himself and the entryway carpet. That made for a great introduction. Little did I know how descriptive our first interaction would be of the rest of our friendship: caffeinated and a bit messy. I walked in right in time to witness the spill, so it was great timing to help with the clean up. Service was starting and I could tell he was new and nervous, so I assured him I'd take care of the mess and sent him in to find a seat. I sopped up the mess, scrubbed the carpet for a couple minutes, then grabbed my Bible and notes as I caught the tail end of worship before I went up to preach. He told me later how shocked he was to see the guy who helped him clean up his coffee walk onto the stage to preach!

There was something about Alex I was drawn to and it wasn't long until we went from spilling coffee to drinking coffee together. Being brand new to following Jesus, he was wide-eyed and excited about his new relationship and the way God was changing him. He came from a gnarly past (in his words), overdosing three times, almost dying in a motorcycle accident, then getting out of the Army after his relationship with his wife fell apart. He had survived overdoses, dodged jail time, and attended the funerals of ten of his friends in three years. He had done basically every stupid thing possible to get himself killed or jailed and it hadn't worked, so there had to be a reason he was sitting in front of me at C3 Coffee in downtown Clarksville. As we sat across the wobbly metal table from each other, him talking, me squinting to keep the blinding sunlight out of my eyes, both of us sweating as we drank piping hot Americanos, I knew this was right. Alex was searching, but not like he had been for most of his life. Before I met him, he had spent years searching for the next high, the next girl, and the next dollar. No more. That was in the past. This was a new, purpose-filled search, but it was a search nonetheless. He didn't know where to go with his life or what he was supposed to be doing. All he had was a phrase he kept circling back to: "I gotta tell somebody." He told me that when I first met with him in my office, and he'd remind me of it often when we got together. He wasn't even entirely sure what it meant or who exactly the "somebody" was, but he knew this was his mission - telling people about the newfound hope he had in Jesus.

I hope you meet an Alex one day. His or her name will probably be different as will their circumstances, but they will help and encourage you. As much as God used me to speak into Alex's life, God used Alex to speak into mine.

One day as I was getting ready to meet up with him, three words came to mind that I knew were for Alex, but I had no idea how deeply they would end up impacting both of our lives. Now years later, they are words I live by and share with people regularly. They are the three words this chapter is about.

I believe following God and living in His will is as simple as the three words God gave me that day. To be clear, "simple" is different than "easy." Following and living in God's will is simple because there are only three words in three steps. But it's far from easy because living these words out will be a lifelong journey you will fail at regularly.

Here they are:
Prayerful.
Faithful.
Available.

If we will live lives defined by those three words, it will remove us from the frustrating scavenger hunt of "finding God's will" and put us directly within His will! God's will isn't something we need to constantly be searching for; it's something we should be constantly living in.

"

God's will isn't something we need to
constantly be searching for; it's something we should be constantly living in.

Let's unpack those three simple words together:

PRAYERFUL

A prayerful life is a conversational life. It's a life that is constantly
diving deeper into a relationship with God through deep, consistent
conversation with Him. This means constantly asking God what
He wants and telling Him what you need as you go. In the church
world, you'll often hear the phrase "prayer life." Although I try to
steer clear of Christianese words and phrases like "quiet time,"
"hedge of protection," and "unspoken" prayer requests, I like the
phrase "prayer life" because I think it captures the idea of what
God wants for us. He doesn't want prayer to be just something we
do, but instead, a way of life. If we tried to breathe only once in
the morning for a few minutes each day then go on with our lives
without worrying about breathing, we wouldn't make it to lunch or
even to work that day. Spiritually speaking, it's the same with prayer.
E.M. Bounds said, "Every day spent in prayerlessness is a day spent
in functional atheism."1

Prayer is to the Christian what breathing is to our body: it
keeps us alive and growing. Just as breaths are going in and out
of your lungs right now as you are reading this, prayers should be
consistently going in and out of our hearts. "Pray without ceasing"
(1 Thessalonians 5:17 ESV) may sound like an intimidating command,
but don't be scared. Just as Nehemiah prayed for most of the
first chapter of his book, he also muttered one- and two-sentence
prayers under his breath throughout the book. Channel your inner
Nehemiah and cultivate a habit of both in your life.

In the ministry world, this means prayerfully considering
every decision from the start and along the way: where you're
planting, who you're empowering for ministry, how your team and
church are going to run, and all of the other thousands of details
you'll need to consider along the way. If you are consistent with
asking, you can rest assured God will be consistent with answering!

It's one of my favorite promises in Scripture: James 1:5 reassures us, "If any of you lacks wisdom, let him ask of God who gives liberally and without reproach." It turns out our problem is not a lack of wisdom, it's often our refusal to ask.

If you are consistent with asking, you can rest assured God will be consistent with answering!

My mom is an amazing example of prayer. I love that she attends and serves at our church, leading The Prayer Hub, one of close to twenty ministry teams people can serve on. She is organized and faithful in her prayers. She keeps records of what she is praying for, Bible verses that go along with her prayers, and will periodically reach out and ask for updates. And she doesn't just pray a couple times. There are many things she's been praying for for years! She is one of the best living examples of living a prayerful life I know.

Pastors, we cannot afford to lead strategic, professional, excellent churches that are void of prayer. A church that is void of prayer is void of power. A church that is void of power will eventually cease to be a church. After all, if the Church is the body of Christ, but is not communicating with Christ, what does that make us? Like a husband and wife that live in the same home, but don't share finances or talk, a Christian and church that doesn't stay in communication with God is heading nowhere but down.

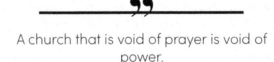

A church that is void of prayer is void of power.

I imagine almost everyone reading a book like this would say prayer is powerful, but I wonder how often our lives and prayers actually reflect that. Think about prayer for a moment: it gives us a direct line to the Creator of the universe. Rarely will you get a chance to talk with a powerful CEO or business owner who can make big decisions. Even if you do get to, your time will most likely be scheduled and brief. Not with God. Anytime. Anywhere. Any topic. Just open your mouth (or your heart if you can't pray out loud) and talk to the Creator of the universe. Let that breathe life and power into your prayers.

Keep in the front of your mind the reality that anything that is hard or impossible for you, He has already done something infinitely more impossible, and He did it with ease. Before the atoms and molecules had ever come together to form creation and when the world was completely pitch black - darker than any dark we have ever experienced - God spoke the word "light," and blinding light pierced the darkness. In a fraction of a second, something that had never existed suddenly did. And He didn't even give the atoms and molecules instructions; they just formed whatever He spoke. He didn't have to speak instructions because He speaks in solutions. It's the God who did *that* that you are talking to in prayer! Think about that next time when you are praying for a new building, the finances of your church, the salvation of a family member, a new venture God seems to be leading you toward, or some seemingly impossible issue you're convinced will never happen. Anything you can possibly dream up, God has already topped. You can't out-dream His creativity or out-pray His power.

Anything you can possibly dream up,
God has already topped. You can't
out-dream His creativity or out-pray
His power.

Prayer not only harnesses the power of God, it also prepares us for the answer. When we are praying expectantly for something, our ears and eyes are open for the answer. We are constantly scanning circumstances and exploring options, expecting God to answer. When we're praying consistently and in faith, prayer keeps us in a constant state of expectation. And since we're always on the lookout, waiting for an answer, we are ready to take the next step of faith because we are expecting God to lead us!

As Martin Luther so eloquently put it, "Prayer is not overcoming God's reluctance; it is laying hold of His willingness." When you pray for God to build His church, expand the reach of the Gospel, bring in leaders, and pour out His Spirit, you should pray in confidence and great faith because those are exactly the prayers God wants to answer. He's just been waiting for someone to ask!

FAITHFUL

Of the three words I'm sharing with you in this chapter, this second one may be the most overlooked. We understand the need to be *prayerful,* and especially when it's hard, we're *available* for the next assignment. But there's a big need for us to be *faithful* right where we are.

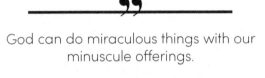

God can do miraculous things with our minuscule offerings.

At Awaken, we regularly say, *"We use what's in our hands."* Like the boy who gave Jesus his loaves and fishes and the widow who gave her two mites to the Lord, we know God can do miraculous things with our minuscule offerings. If we will just be willing to trust God with what we have, He'll take care of the rest. And by the way, the irony of "being faithful with what we have" is that in reality, we are just trusting God to be faithful with what He entrusted us with. David spoke of this at the end of 1 Chronicles when he gave a large portion from his own treasury to fund the Lord's work. He was humbled and amazed that he had the honor to give to the Lord what was actually the Lord's in the first place. He says,

> **"But who am I, and what is my people, that we should be able thus to offer willingly? For all things come from you, and of your own have we given you. O Lord our God, all this abundance that we have provided for building you a house for your holy name comes from your hand and is all your own."**
> **(1 Chronicles 29:14,16 ESV)**

Think of the irony and humbling perspective this provides.

The building you're struggling to be content with? That's God's building. He entrusted it into your care. Be faithful with it.

The budget you're constantly saying isn't enough? That's God's money. He entrusted you with it and expects you to be faithful with it.

The people who rub you the wrong way, push your buttons, and seem to instinctively know the perfect time to say the wrong thing? They're God's people. He made sure they were under your care, at least for this season. Be faithful to take care of them.

The stress that's constantly on your mind, keeping you awake at night? That's God's stress, actually. Give it back to Him! The good thing is, He doesn't slumber or sleep. Since He's going to be up anyway, go get some rest! Be faithful. God's got you.

He doesn't slumber or sleep. Since He's going to be up anyway, go get some rest!

God's building. God's money. God's people. When you remember *Whose* they are, it helps you remember *who* you are. In light of that truth, faithfulness in your calling is less a command and more the logical response to a gracious God.

Faithfulness isn't a season and it isn't a feeling; it's a decision we make despite how we feel.

Church planting, pastoring, and following Jesus in general will be filled with many seasons that are not easy and where you're tempted to quit (for us, the entire first year of church planting, as well as the third, the eighth, and the ninth so far), but you are called to be faithful anyway. Faithfulness isn't a season and it isn't a feeling; it's a decision we make despite how we feel.

This is why Paul reminds Timothy to preach the word in season and out of season (2 Timothy 4 ESV). I love the "in season" preaching! The crowd is engaged - Bibles open, pens out, shouting me down... Those are great times, but they're not all the time. In fact, that can change from weekend to weekend, and sometimes from service to service on a Sunday, or even from one part of the service to the next. It's wildly unpredictable. "In season" preaching is the fun stuff that energizes me. It's the "out of season" preaching and leading that's hard. As I mentioned earlier, there have been Sundays that if it weren't for the fact that I was the pastor and was supposed to preach that day, I would have stayed in bed and not gone to church. In fact, out of rebellion, I wouldn't have even live-streamed the service from home (gasp!). The "out of season" leadership is why Paul compares the work of ministry to the hard work and faithfulness of a soldier, a farmer, and an athlete. Don't give up. Stay faithful. It takes dedication and discipline, but God honors faithfulness.

I once heard someone say, "I resolved early on not to take it personally when the church isn't growing because then when it does grow, I'll be tempted to take the credit." Taking it personally and taking the credit are both things you should resist at all costs. That doesn't mean you shouldn't evaluate your leadership. Evaluating and making course changes along the way is healthy, wise, and a sign of good leadership. In fact, it's part of being faithful. This should, however, be a reminder that just because your church isn't growing doesn't mean you're failing. Remember that the church is a body. Just as our physical bodies grow at different rates and through different spurts, the church does the same. There have been seasons we have seen our church simultaneously shrink numerically while growing in depth and generosity. Don't define "growth" in your church only by shallow numerical statistics. Numbers are important, but they're not the only important thing or even the most important.

One of our favorite compliments we hear from people who visit our church or tour our buildings is that we use our space very creatively and efficiently. From adding a second worship space to accommodate growth to squeezing kids into small classrooms and using offices for counseling and nursing mothers, we use rooms and spaces for many creative purposes.

We've been live-streaming our Sunday services since 2014 and have seen people from eighty-eight countries tune in and many make faith decisions while watching online! Some people may assume that with a global reach like that, we must have a pretty big broadcasting team and space with an elaborate setup. Not exactly. Our Media Team Leader, Jacob, has done a phenomenal job using to max capacity the space we have. Every Sunday, he and one or two other team members sit in a six-foot by six-foot room to broadcast the message around the world. The room used to be our janitorial supply closet, but today the mops have been replaced with monitors, the buckets with control boards, and the supplies with video switches. Everywhere I look, there is high tech stuff that is above my pay grade. The room is so tight and jammed so full that I have to watch my head when I walk in. Standing in the middle with outstretched arms, I can touch all four walls without moving! Eighty-eight countries have been reached from a thirty-six square foot janitor-closet-turned-broadcast-room. More countries than square feet! That is faithfulness!

Jacob and his team have done an incredible job of being faithful with what's in their hands. We dream of the day when we can spread out and go big, but we're not going to let what we want distract or deter us from being faithful with what we have.

We're not going to let what we want distract or deter us from being faithful with what we have.

Because Clarksville is near Ft. Campbell, the nation's second largest Army post, Awaken Church tends to run about sixty percent military families. Our desire to be faithful greatly impacts how we minister to our military families. Since most Army families are only with us for two to three years, it would be easy for us to resist investing in them. We view their fleeting time with us in the opposite way. It doesn't push us away; it encourages us to invest more and quicker, since our time with them is so limited.

God has honored that investment. We now have dozens of families who have put their faith in Christ at Awaken, then moved to all parts of the nation and the world, taking their newfound faith with them. Although we could bemoan their departure, we choose to rejoice! Rarely does a ten-year old church have missionaries on multiple continents, paid for by the government! Thanks, Uncle Sam!

Being faithful with what we have doesn't mean not wanting or even asking for more. Admittedly, this can be a weird, blurry line to walk. Here's how this may sound in prayer: "God, I'm so thankful for the building, budget, and people You've already provided me with. I'll use what You've given us for Your glory in the most strategic ways that I can. I'm also asking that You would help us to effectively and strategically reach even more people, whether that's with what You've already provided or with something new You'll give us sometime soon. Either way, I trust You and only want what You want."

Whatever you have and in whatever you do, live faithful. Nobody ever regretted being faithful.

AVAILABLE

Being available to God is something many church planters and people in ministry are well aware of. You sensed God's calling to launch out, and if anything, it wasn't so much availability you lacked, it was patience. "God, I'll go right now," you may have said. Availability plays out in many different ways, though. Staying available to God isn't just about moving onto something new, it's also about being open-handed with everything God has given you. In addition, availability is about trusting God when He calls you to step into something really hard: a tough conversation, a challenging decision, or a blind step of faith.

My wife, Jenn, lived this out with a ministry she launched at Awaken called Revive. Around the year six mark of our church, she and a team of women spent a year praying about the timing and logistics of launching a women's gathering at our church. God rewarded their patience and prayerfulness and the launch of Revive was clearly Spirit-led. She ran Revive for a couple years, always available to the leading of the Spirit, praying as she went. One thing we work hard at doing at Awaken is making sure we don't do things just to do things. When we question why we are doing something, if the answer is anywhere near, "Because that's how we've always done it," then we end it. That's a bad reason to do anything, and it's the opposite of being available, as we are discussing.

Over the course of four years, Revive went through many changes: they started meeting on Saturday mornings once per month, then moved to Monday evenings once monthly. They provided childcare for a few semesters, then removed it. They eventually moved to meeting eight months out of the year on

Monday nights and most recently changed to four quarterly events. The changes had nothing to do with them being fickle or indecisive; they made changes as they listened and stayed available to the Lord's leading, constantly doing their best to meet the needs of the women they were ministering to. Trust me. I heard the behind-the-scenes conversations and saw the tears as they worked through the frustration and logistics. There were things they wanted to do that just didn't seem right as they continued to pray, and there were changes that felt odd to implement that in hindsight were exactly what needed to happen. In so many ways, Jenn and her leadership team exemplify the principle of Proverbs 16:9 ESV, "Man plans his ways, but the Lord directs his steps."

If you want a Bible verse that sums up availability, there it is. Thank you very much, Solomon.

"Man plans his way."

Availability isn't indecisiveness and it certainly is not a lack of planning. Keep planning! Staying available to God's leading does not mean you pray about something then kick up your feet and wait for Him to do it. Staying available is an active thing, just as true, faith-filled prayer is meant to be. God is sovereign over the details, but God's sovereignty never negates our responsibility.

God is sovereign over the details, but God's sovereignty never negates our responsibility.

"But the Lord directs his steps."

Plan big and be detailed. When it comes to church planting and pastoring, pick a city, set a date, build a team, rent a building, start teams, launch small groups… Make plans, but don't marry your plans. Don't commit your life to them and don't write them in stone. Being available means letting the Lord direct your steps. Our plans should be in pencil and God's direction etched in stone.

Living a life that is available to God means presenting your life, family, and ministry to God every day and telling Him, "God, do what you want in us and through us. We are yours." I have a pastor friend who annually fasts and prays with his wife about whether or not they should continue on at their church for another year.

For decades, the answer was yes. Then one year as they prayed, something seemed different. They had three kids, two of which were teenagers at the time. Leaving stability and launching out was scary and didn't make a lot of sense, but they were available if that was God's desire. As they followed God's direction, within a calendar year they had transitioned the church to a new leader and planted a new one. Five years in, they have a few thousand in attendance across two campuses. That is being available!

―――――――― 99 ――――――――

Hands that are open to God's direction
are also open for God's provision.

――――――――――――――――

Keep your hands open. So many of us have a white-knuckle grip on our plans, hopes, and dreams. When we are willing to trust God's love, wisdom, and sovereignty, it will help us open our sweaty hands and release our plans to God. When our hands are open, God has free reign over our plans and can direct us as He sees fit. There's an added benefit too: hands that are open to God's direction are also open for God's provision. When we white-knuckle-grip our plans, our fists are closed to God's provision and blessing. When we open them up and become more flexible with our future, our hands are open for God to pour His blessings into.

Prayerful.
Faithful.
Available.

They belong in that order.

Prayer should not be our last resort; it should be our first response. If we are constantly prayerful, only then can we be fully faithful, as prayer gives us the strength and direction to carry on no matter what. Only once we are prayerful and faithful can we be available for whatever God has next.

Back to Alex.

It didn't take long for Satan to entice Alex with a paycheck and a romanticized version of life back where he grew up in Myrtle Beach. I reminded him of those three words: prayerful, faithful, available. After a lot of intense deliberation and prayer, he took a step of faith and stayed in Clarksville. That decision changed the course of his life. He met his future wife here, we hired him at our church, and he eventually moved across the nation and attended the same ministry school I had attended fourteen years prior. He had rarely succeeded at anything in life, but he worked hard in School of Ministry. I surprised him by flying in for his graduation ceremony, where I got to deliver the commencement speech. I spoke three words to Alex and his graduating class that night: "If you want to know God's will for your life and your calling for ministry, stay prayerful, faithful, and available."

99

If we will live lives that are prayerful, faithful, and available, we will no longer have to search for God's will, we will be living directly in it!

If we will live lives that are *prayerful, faithful, and available*, we will no longer have to search for God's will, we will be living directly in it!

There it is. I wrote 4,700 words in order to share three words with you. I hope they change your life and ministry as they have mine. In fact, I hope they fill you with faith as God leads you to trust Him even when that next step feels crazy.

NINE

39° IN THE POURING RAIN

The line between faith and stupid is often blurry.

Any time we tell people we need a bigger building because we're out of space, they're often quick to say, "Well that's a good problem!" It's true. It is a good problem. It's still a problem, though. Since the very beginning, space has been an issue for our church. In ten years, counting the living room we started in, we've rented or met in five different buildings. And the current one we're in started with us renting 2,400 square feet and has now led to us owning all 32,000 square feet spread across three buildings sitting on six acres!

Sometimes I have a hard time trying to figure out if I'm being faithful or stupid. The struggle is real. Maybe you can relate.

CODE NAME "JERICHO"

Clarksville Building and Codes told us "no" to building out or renovating our shopping center on Riverside Drive for years. They seemed to use the word "no" like my father-in-law says I use salt: way too early and way too much. Our church campus and venues are pretty unique. We added a second venue on our campus under the same roof before we even owned the shopping center. I preach in the "North Venue" and we have live worship and a live-synced video of the teaching in the "South Venue." Each venue seats 110, which worked well for a while, but we've long since outgrown it and needed something new.

Cue the bluelight special.

Kmart went out of business in 2016 and as we walked the aisles browsing their eighty percent off "everything must go, including the shelves and fixtures" sale, Jenn and I talked about how great it would be to turn that huge building into a church one day. For awhile, we tried unsuccessfully to figure out who owned it and how to contact them about selling.

For the next two years, it just sat there. Hundreds of fluorescent lights inside lit up the 90,000-square-foot building, giving it a yellow glow and the hum of flowing electricity. Weeds grew all around it, plastic newspaper stands dry-rotted in the sunlight, and the back of the building became a local secret trash dump. You never knew what you'd find back there: an old TV, cans of cat food spread around to feed the herd of feral cats, or even dozens of old, broken couches, accent chairs, and coffee tables. That's not to mention the old gas station out front, complete with its own weeds, fading paint, and humming fluorescent lights illuminating refrigerators that were once filled with thirty flavors of Gatorade and overpriced gallons of milk.

It was an eyesore. A beautiful, 90,000 square feet, empty canvas eyesore. I thought about it every once in a while as I would drive by multiple times per week on my way to church or heading home.

Two years later, in the beginning of 2018, I met Tommy. He is a well-connected leader in our community, grew up in New Mexico (which makes us homies), spent some time in jail, and barely escaped prison time back in the day. I've been with him before at church when people recognize him from his tattoos while his hands are lifted in worship. If he finds out you're from New Mexico, he'll yell, "505 represent!" and give you a big hug while asking you when you ate green chile enchiladas last. I love being around Tommy. His energy and enthusiasm for life and Jesus are contagious. At the time when he visited Awaken Church, he was serving as the County Commissioner for Montgomery County. Sometimes God brings unexpected people into your life you didn't know you needed to know. Tommy would become a godsend of connection and encouragement for me.

After church that Sunday, I reached out to Tommy to see if he knew anything about the Kmart owner. Within an hour, I was on an email string with the county mayor with contact info for the real estate agent and a promise from the mayor that he would do anything he could to help! After two years of reaching out, the door seemed to be opening. Our realtor tried for the next week to get in touch with the agent, and when she finally heard back, the door was shut. Their agent worked in Nashville and did not want to "waste" his time driving to Clarksville to open the building for a church that probably couldn't afford to buy the building anyway. I was discouraged by the response, but excited that we had finally made contact.

As I drove by later that day, I stopped at a red light at the intersection nearby and looked over at Kmart as I had done a hundred times before. Sitting at a red light carried with it a sense of irony. Red lights seemed to be all we had received so far. It was in that moment that I prayed a simple prayer. I said, "God, if You could get Israel into Jericho, you can get Awaken into Kmart. Show us what You can do." My prayer was that simple. No tongues or prophecy or tears or warm feelings. Just a simple prayer of faith, asking God to do what we had not been able to do for years. Never underestimate the power of prayer. When we pray, God moves.

99

Never underestimate the power of
prayer. When we pray, God moves.

As I finished that prayer, I felt this nudge to pay attention to the time. I glanced down at the neon green digital clock in my SUV. It was 4:23 pm. When I got home, I had a text from Tommy saying he was on the phone with the agent and I should pray. The text had come in at 4:23 as I sat at that red light praying to get in. I wrote it in my prayer journal and shared that bit of news with my wife, excited but having no real connection to 4:23. Yet.

As Jenn was driving home later that day with the kids, she texted me, "Meet me at Jericho." Ten minutes later, we met in the Kmart parking lot.

I remember pulling into that lot that morning. The lot was empty, but I was full of faith and vision. I hadn't dreamed like this in a while and my sails felt fuller than they had in a long time. I parked my car, got into our SUV with my wife and kids, then it got real.

Parked outside of Kmart with rain gently hitting the windshield, Jenn told me, "When you said you prayed that prayer at 4:23, I immediately thought you were going to say to read Joshua 4:23. I don't know why, but that was immediately the thought I had. I just read it and you have to read it! Look it up!"

I pulled out my phone, opened the Bible app, and flipped as quickly as I could to Joshua 4. Here are the words that leapt off my screen at me:

> **"For the Lord your God dried up the waters of the Jordan for you until you passed over, as the Lord your God did to the Red Sea, which he dried up for us until we passed over, so that all the peoples of the earth may know that the hand of the Lord is mighty, that you may fear the Lord your God forever.""**
> **(Joshua 4:23-24 ESV)**

For the previous few weeks, I had been led to pray Nehemiah 6:16 ESV, that God would do a work in and through us and everyone watching would "perceive that this work had been accomplished with the help of our God." Now Joshua 4:23-24 was saying the same thing! In addition, Joshua 4 was not only relating Israel's story, it was talking about our story too: God had dried up the flood that had once overwhelmed us as well!

Our minds blown and hearts full, we began doing what everyone knows you do at Jericho: circling and praying. The sun was obscured by clouds, rain fell as we drove, but we prayed with faith and anticipation! As we circled four tenths of a mile around the building each time, something lying in the parking lot caught my eye. I asked Jenn to stop the car on our next lap around the building and I jumped out to get a closer look. I couldn't believe my eyes.

"Jenn, you're gonna want to see this!" I yelled. There in the drizzling rain, lying in the back of this old Kmart building, we gathered around the object I had seen. It was a Bible, lying open to Deuteronomy 30. The pages bent, ripped, folded, and stuck together, only two verses were legible on both pages:

> **"I call heaven and earth to witness against you today, that I have set before you life and death, blessing and curse. Therefore choose life, that you and your offspring may live, loving the Lord your God, obeying his voice and holding fast to him, for he is your life and length of days, that you may dwell in the land that the Lord swore to your fathers, to Abraham, to Isaac, and to Jacob, to give them."**
> **(Deuteronomy 30:19-20 ESV)**

My preacher mind immediately put that verse into its proper context. These were God's words through Moses to the nation of Israel as they overlooked the land God had promised to give them!

He was reminding them to trust Him and hold firm to their faith so He could provide the land they were looking at!

We couldn't believe our eyes. Our hoodies soaked with rain and tears, we scooped up the soaking Bible, put it in the back of our vehicle and kept lapping and praying, faith and anticipation growing by the minute. I told Jenn, "This is no longer just some land we are hoping to get. This is our promised land. This is our Canaan. Our Jericho. We are going to pray and fight for this land until it's ours."

I texted the other pastors and their wives and said to meet us at the building that afternoon at 4:23 pm so we could pray. I shared the story with them, showed them the Bible, and we walked more laps praying for God's provision.

OUT IN THE OPEN

God-given vision, in its infant state, has to be protected and guarded. Just as Nehemiah prayed and fasted for months and even circled Jerusalem multiple times before sharing the vision to rebuild, we did the same. We kept it to ourselves for the next couple weeks until the time was right to share with the staff. On Monday morning a few weeks later, I texted the staff the address and told them we'd be interrupting our regularly scheduled Tuesday morning team meetup.

God-given vision, in its infant state, has
to be protected and guarded.

I remember pulling into the parking lot that Tuesday morning. The sight of the staff standing at the front of the building and their cars filling up the front dozen or so parking spaces filled me with expectation and faith! I shared the story with them and showed them the Bible I had brought with me, now dry, crisp, and fragile. We walked a couple laps as we prayed, then stopped at the loading dock behind the building, put our hands on the building, and prayed. It was monumental.

I asked them to keep it quiet until the time was right, which was only a few weeks later. After a few weeks of still not being able to get in to tour it and rumors of multiple other offers swirling, I decided it was time to get the whole church praying. After weeks of keeping this exciting secret quiet, Jenn and I shared the vision with the church and showed them the Bible we had found. Then I told them, "We're going to do something crazy today. We are going to go to that old Kmart building this evening at 6:00 pm and worship and pray in that parking lot like it belongs to us!" At every service, people stood and clapped and cheered, elated and filled with faith about the possibilities and God's provision so far.

We prayed for the clouds to part and the sun to shine, but when 5:45 pm rolled around, we bundled up in winter coats and rain gear and braced ourselves for the cold front. It was 39 degrees and raining, so the chances of people actually showing up to pray seemed slim, but we would be there, even if it was just us and a dozen others!

I wasn't prepared for the sight we saw when we rolled into the parking lot that day. Braving the downpour and almost freezing temperatures, families and people had driven from all around Clarksville and surrounding communities, bundled up in winter coats, gloves, blankets, and galoshes, carrying umbrellas. Moms pushed strollers with kids bundled up under layers of blankets and people wrapped their faces to keep in the warmth as much as they could. We parked and walked into one of the strongest feelings of faith and anticipation we had ever experienced. We could see our breath as we prayed and worshiped. I spoke from Joshua 6 about worshiping and shouting because God had given Jericho to Israel... even before it looked like He had!

We sang an Awaken Worship Project original, "My God Is Able."

> *"I will trust in You, You will see me through,*
> *I will trust in You, My God is able.*
> *I will trust in You, I will not be moved,*
> *I will trust in You, My God is able."*

Our Worship Director, Kelly, wrote those lyrics in a very trying season we had weathered a year prior. Words that helped carry us through that dark season took on new meaning as we faced this new challenge.

And of course we had to sing Elevation Worship's song, "Do It Again."[1]

"Walking around these walls
I thought by now they'd fall
But You have never failed me yet
Waiting for change to come
Knowing the battle's won
For You have never failed me yet

I've seen You move, come move the mountains
And I believe, I'll see You do it again"

I have never experienced faith and worship like I did that day. God's presence was tangible and the atmosphere was electric.

PRAYER SPIES

We had tried for two years to get in to tour that building, but to no avail. We had been trying even harder for the last six weeks and still had no luck. On the following Monday morning, fifteen hours after our freezing cold, drenched-by-rain-and-the-Spirit worship and prayer concert in the parking lot, I got a phone call from our realtor. We were in! The agent had changed his mind and agreed to drive to Clarksville to let us into the building! Just like that, our worship and prayer had shaken something loose.

I told the staff we were heading into Jericho the next morning and they had a special role. I told them that I, our realtor, and a couple other local business owner friends of mine would walk around with the agent, but the staff was the team of Joshua and Caleb prayer spies. I equipped them with a couple vials of anointing oil, and as I talked with the agent, the prayer spies deployed, covering all 90,000 square feet in prayer and worship.

Our kids had been with us every step thus far, so we pulled them out of school for the morning to join us. Our youngest daughter, Adalyn, seven years old at the time, suddenly got sick and threw up in the backseat of the car as they drove to Kmart. Jenn knew she needed to get Adalyn home, meaning she would miss the walk-through. Not on Adalyn's watch! She refused to let some nausea cause her to miss this miracle. Jenn borrowed a shirt from my mom, Adalyn changed clothes, and she walked into that Kmart pale-faced and praying by faith...in grandma's baggy t-shirt.

At first, it had felt stupid to pray for this building. But this? This was what faith felt like!

A FAMILIAR TENSION

However, as can be expected, like the paint on the outside of the abandoned Kmart building, the feeling of faith eventually began to fade.

Snarky comments and swirling doubt began to find their way back into my mind...

The real estate agent had laughed at us when we said we believe God was going to give us the building. He said, "Well we have a couple high dollar offers already, so it will have to be God for you to get it!"

As we were about to walk in to tour the building, a friend of mine and local business owner told me that going inside with our church staff was "real estate suicide." He told me the agent wanted us there in order to force his other buyer to make a move.

Banks weren't real interested in talking to an eight-year old church about a multi-million dollar loan.

It was already a miracle for us to own a shopping center we bought for $1.6 million, but getting another shopping center for $3 million?! How would we pull that off?

For months afterward, I felt so conflicted when we would drive around the vacant building to pray. Some days, I was soaring with faith, believing for miracles and praying for God to do abundantly beyond what we could imagine. Other days, I felt discouraged and overwhelmed. The questions of "how" and "what if" started to creep in, and I'd wonder if I was crazy for doing this or at least crazy for going public with this.

That tension was familiar. I had felt it before.

Uprooting my family and moving across the country with a two-year old and my six-months pregnant wife to plant a church? That seemed stupid to me at times as well as to others. I had job offers, crying friends and family, and we were leaving behind an incredible community. Looking back, I know it was faith. There were plenty of signs along the way. But in the middle of it, it didn't always feel like faith. It often felt kind of stupid.

Starting a church from scratch in a city we'd never lived in with people we'd never met? What were we thinking?! I didn't have a job, but I did have three mouths to feed (including mine) and another mouth on the way!

When I look back, I could list many more examples of steps of faith that felt stupid mid-step.

Looking back and seeing God's faithfulness play out as the details fall into place is great, but you may be right in the middle of it right now, unable to look back just yet.

It's easy for us to cheer Joseph on in Genesis 37 when he's shared his vision of his brothers' sheaves bowing down to his — we know the rest of the story. "Hang on, Joseph! Your brothers are jerks, but God's got you! It's all going to work out! I read chapter 50 already" we think as we read those climactic chapters.

The problem is, we may feel like we are living in Genesis 37. We can't see the next chapter, much less the next page. Is it stupid to hold onto that crazy vision we thought was from the Lord, especially when those closest to us think we are stupid?

WHICH ONE IS IT?

Is this what faith feels like or am I stupid?

Whether you're a pastor, church planter, or a Christian trying to follow Jesus further, here are a few ways you can learn to distinguish between stupid and faith...

When you know God is leading, IT'S FAITH.

There will be times throughout your life and ministry, where you know God is leading you to do something that seems crazy...like plant a church, start a new ministry team, do something in a way you've never seen it done, or some other scary step of faith. Faith by definition is crazy. It's stepping into the unknown. It's "the conviction of things not seen," according to Hebrews 11:1 ESV. Whether God leads you through His Word, prayer, circumstance, or however, when He's leading, keep walking, even when it feels crazy. Negative opinions will abound and haters will share their unsolicited opinions, but if God is for us, who can be against us (Romans 8:31 ESV)?

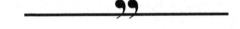

Faith by definition is crazy. It's stepping
into the unknown.

When your motives are selfish, IT'S STUPID.

God will never lead you to do something where you get the credit instead of Him. He doesn't share His glory and He didn't put you into ministry or give you a platform so you could become famous. If building a giant church is your endgame, that's selfish and stupid. A giant church is the byproduct of reaching the lost, not the goal. God never rewards selfish ambition and personal glory. Seeking fame is not only stupid, it is self-sabotaging.

God will never lead you to do something where you get the credit instead of Him.

When people think you're stupid, it may be FAITH.
One name: Noah.

He knew God was leading him. Regardless of what people thought, he went ahead and built that giant, floating petting zoo in his front yard amidst the mockery of the onlookers and the protests of his H.O.A. We sold our condo when our moving truck was halfway packed. We left a community and well-paying job to move to a city with neither. Years later, we marched around that vacant Kmart building in 39 degrees and pouring rain. People thought we were crazy for all of that and more. It's much easier to criticize someone for doing something crazy than to get out and do something! At times, God will use people to direct you, but at other times, the devil will use people to distract you. Make sure God's voice is the loudest.

God will use people to direct you, but at other times, the devil will use people to distract you. Make sure God's voice is the loudest.

When people think you're stupid, you may be STUPID.
There are plenty of times where I should have listened to the people around me, but for whatever reason, I forged ahead and regretted it. There have been times where I ignored Jenn's God-given gift of

discernment and it came back to bite me. At other times, I pushed forward with a decision and ended up inadvertently hurting feelings or injuring relationships. When you consistently surround yourself with Godly voices and the combined chorus of their voices is telling you not to go forward with something, pay attention. Proverbs reminds us that "faithful are the wounds of a friend" (Proverbs 27:6 ESV) and "in a multitude of counselors there is safety" (Proverbs 11:14 NKJV). Make sure God's voice is the loudest, but the voices of the Godly people you've surrounded yourself with should be only slightly quieter than His.

JUST BUILD THE BOAT

What if you planted a church and there were only fourteen people in attendance at the ten-year birthday? That was the case with a friend of mine who launched out to plant a church a few years before I did. I spent years talking with him, encouraging him, praying for him, and helping him brainstorm strategic ways to grow the church he had planted.

There were times where his faith was soaring and other times where he didn't know how much longer he could go on. I couldn't blame him.

I often didn't have answers for him and I could never really put a finger on what was preventing the growth of his church. But there was one thing I knew that I constantly reminded him of: God wasn't after his church's attendance; He was after his obedience.

When the time came for him to transition the church to someone else, I affirmed to him over and over that he had succeeded at church planting. Success was not a huge church. Success was huge obedience even when the results were underwhelming.

Speaking of faithfulness, here's a crazy thought: what if God had never flooded the earth like He told Noah He was going to? Would Noah still have received God's blessing?

In other words, was Noah's blessing from God contingent on the fulfillment of God's promise or the obedience of Noah's faith?

I would argue it's the latter.

Sometimes my wife drops nuggets of gold on me like this from her time in the Word. She shared this one with me recently after reading about Noah in Hebrews 11. That's one of the many benefits of spending regular time in God's Word. When you get into God's Word, it gets into you and empowers you, encourages you, and convicts you right when you need it most.

The Bible says Noah "became an heir of the righteousness that comes by faith" (Hebrews 11:7 ESV). His blessing wasn't contingent on the flood; it was contingent on his faith and his subsequent obedience.

I want an extra helping of faith like Noah. He was willing to do what God told him to do even though those around him—and maybe even his family—thought he was off his rocker.

Had it never flooded, he still would have been rewarded because he obeyed.

If we never get Kmart, I know I responded in faith and God will reward that.

Your reward isn't subject to the fulfillment of God's promise. That's His end of the deal to hold up. You are simply responsible for obeying no matter how difficult, impossible, or crazy it seems.

We tend to define the success of a step of faith by the fulfillment of the promise, but this perspective puts a new spin on the definition of success and failure. "Failure" in the world's eyes is often success in God's eyes because it was never about the outcome to begin with it. It was always about the obedience.

"Failure" in the world's eyes is often success in God's eyes because it was never about the outcome to begin with it. It was always about the obedience.

CONTENT AND DISSATISFIED

I believe the tension between faith and stupid is often due to the balance between contentment and dissatisfaction.

Here's how we say it at Awaken: *We will always be content with our resources but never satisfied with our reach.*

Contentment is a spiritual mindset that rests in God's sovereignty and provision. Contentment says, "If I don't have it, I don't need it. And when I need it, God will provide it." Contentment isn't searching for some secret sauce that will finally do the trick. Contentment says, "God, all I have is these five loaves of bread

COME HELL OR HIGH WATER

and two fish, but I trust You can do incredible things with them." Contentment is the absence of lusting after the next big thing, new trend, or ministry spotlight.

99

> Contentment is a spiritual mindset that rests in God's sovereignty and provision. Contentment says, "If I don't have it, I don't need it. And when I need it, God will provide it."

Dissatisfaction may sound like a bad thing, and I'd agree...if we were talking about a customer service survey. But in our lives, a God-given dissatisfaction is a healthy thing. When we get satisfied, we settle. We buy into the lies that "this is always how it will be," and "I just won't be able to reach those people or take that next step." When we settle for satisfaction, we give up without officially throwing in the towel. We're still showing up each week, preaching, leading, and maybe even smiling, but we've lost the drive to reach further.

Satisfaction is our default. It's Christian cruise control. Cruise control is great in your car, but disastrous for your calling. By the time my pastor was in his mid-sixties and nearing almost forty years as a pastor, he led their church to launch a new campus on the west-side of Albuquerque at the busiest intersection in the city. He is content with his resources, but never satisfied with their reach. I want to be like him when I grow up.

Contentment and dissatisfaction are not mutually exclusive. It's not either/or; it's both/and. You don't have to give up one for the other. In fact, I believe they should coexist in some way in your life, leadership, and church. If you drew a Venn diagram with contentment in one circle and dissatisfaction in the other, your calling is where the two circles intersect. That's the sweet spot where contentment and dissatisfaction go hand in hand.

Paul said, "Godliness with contentment is great gain" (1 Timothy 6:6 ESV). The sooner we can learn to be dissatisfied with our reach, but completely content with our resources, the sooner we can press forward in our faith and see God do the impossible with the little that we have. Just give Him your bread and fish and watch Him feed the crowd!

Want to know what happened with Kmart?

Me too!

We tried to sell Riverside Center and even submitted an offer on the Kmart property, contingent on the sale of our shopping center. I wrote a letter to the Board of Directors of the Sears Holding Company, the owners of Kmart, asking them to consider our offer and/or donate the building to us. I and a few others fasted weekly for most of 2018, believing and praying for the miraculous.

As of the writing of this book, a development company from Chattanooga obtained private funding and purchased the building. Jenn and I attended the groundbreaking ceremony (we were not invited; we just showed up) with the city's elected officials, where they posed for pictures in business attire and hard hats, holding brand new silver shovels. The land and building we are praying for now has fences around it with large, neon yellow "DO NOT ENTER" signs affixed to the fences. Due to the fences, I can no longer drive all the way around the building. Crews have demolished the gas station that came with the Kmart, making room for a new Panera Bread, or so the rumors say. You can see completely through the building now as construction crews have cut gaping holes into the facade of the building to make room for some big box stores they'll be putting in shortly. Marshall's and Burke's have both put "coming soon" signs and banners up in front of their respective storefronts. Time will tell which other chains move in.

I wish I could write an amazing end to the story and say that by the miracle-working hand of God, He shut down the other buyers, provided $3 million in funding for us, contractors donated their time, crews, and materials, and we are holding church in a newly renovated Kmart building.

That's not the story.

Instead, we are still in Riverside Center, the same place we lost everything in the flood in 2010. We are working toward renovating the building there to combine our venues, and are excited about the unity that will bring to our church and teams. I still drive around (or as "around" as I can) the former Kmart building every day I'm in town, which I plan to continue unless God redirects me. As of the publication of this book, I've been praying for 593 days now and have driven at least 300 miles in laps around the building.

In our first few months of praying, someone asked me, "What if it takes ten years till we get Kmart?" I told him a decade of praying daily for a miracle is a decade well spent.

I'm not a flawless example of faith, but I'm trying to walk by faith every day. I still have my days of doubt, especially as the building continues to look less and less like ours. We are holding onto the belief that God has sent construction crews in to do millions of dollars of cleanup work in prep for our future. Sometimes I am full of faith. Other days I feel kind of stupid for still driving around that building.

We don't know what the future holds. Thankfully we know Who holds the future!

"

We don't know what the future holds.
Thankfully we know Who holds the
future!

This is faith. It often feels crazy and I still doubt, but I keep pressing forward, driving laps, and praying big prayers. And as crazy as I feel at times, I have no regrets. We have done everything within our capability to get that building. And since God hasn't provided it for us yet, it's not because He can't, it's because He has a reason to hold off for now. I trust Him either way.

I hope you'll learn to trust Him with your Kmart, too.

TEN

KEEP THE MAIN THING
THE MAIN THING

The gospel is the heartbeat of the Church.

I didn't mean to become a coffee snob. It just kind of happened. Unlike my five-year old, who drinks black Americanos, I didn't even like coffee until I was well into my twenties. Some of our close friends helped me warm up to the idea, then free caramel macchiatos for the pastors at our church cafe was the gateway drug that did me in. I drank girlie, sugared-up, pansy coffee (as my son calls any coffee that's not black) until my laziness got the best of me. Once the macchiatos were no longer free and I was over the work it took to sugar my coffee up, I started weaning myself off of sugar and cream. Eventually, black became my favorite. Like the rest of America, I started purchasing Starbucks beans and brewing my coffee at home in a Mr. Coffee drip brewer. Eventually I got into the world of espresso, again through my friend, Mr. Coffee. But it wasn't until Father's Day of 2016 that everything really changed. That was when Jenn got me an at-home coffee roaster. Well, actually it was a Whirly-Pop stovetop popcorn popper that I converted into a coffee roaster. Pretty quickly I picked up the art of coffee roasting and dove headfirst into it. Before we realized what was happening, my coffee taste buds became too snooty and sophisticated for Starbucks beans and I began shipping in green coffee beans from all over the world: Brazil, South Africa, Mexico, Papua New Guinea... Fast forward a few years, and now we have our own coffee bar in our kitchen, make our own espresso drinks, have taken professional coffee classes, shipped our home-roasted beans to people in more than twenty states and four countries, and own a drip brew coffee maker that has an inch of dust on it.

Here's the point: once you taste the good stuff, you can't go back. Everything else is inferior.

It's the same once you've encountered the life-changing power of solid, biblical teaching.

ALREADY ALL WE NEED

The first ten years of Awaken have often involved taking something old and/or used and retrofitting it to meet our needs: a living room turned into a sanctuary, an old tanning salon, a former cubicle jungle, and a former women's gym. We've taken all of those spaces and more and turned them into something relevant that fit our needs.

But building church buildings isn't the same as building the church. Your church - the local body of believers - isn't founded on or sustained by buildings or the funds that pay for them to be purchased or renovated. The Apostle Paul refers to the church as "the household of God, the church of the living God, a pillar and buttress of the truth" (1 Timothy 3:15 ESV). The global, eternal movement Jesus called the Church is founded on and sustained by the Word of God. How else can we be a pillar and buttress (support) of truth if we are constantly swayed and guided by the fickle opinions of people? As Jesus described, if we build our lives on anything besides Him, our foundation is sinking sand which provides no footing when storms rage. And storms will rage, you can be assured of that.

Unlike a building that needs to be made relevant, God's Word already is relevant. We don't make God's Word relevant; our role is simply to point out and highlight its relevance. God's Word is already all we need.

99

We don't make God's Word relevant;
our role is simply to point out and
highlight its relevance.

Whatever our language, age, or culture, the Bible meets our most basic human needs. God's Word is described as pure spiritual milk (1 Peter 2:2), solid food (Hebrews 5:14), imperishable seed (1 Peter 1:23), truth (John 17:17), a mirror (James 1:25), light (Psalm

119:105), a fire (Jeremiah 5:14), a two-edged sword (Hebrews 4:12), and a hammer (Jeremiah 23:29), to name a few.

Paul told Timothy that all Scripture is inspired. Literally "God-breathed." He said God's Word is "profitable for teaching, for reproof, for correction, and for training in righteousness, that the man of God may be complete, equipped for every good work" (2 Timothy 3:16-17 ESV). The words "all" and "every" may only have a few letters in them, but these are weighty superlatives he is using here.

When he says *all* Scripture, he even means Leviticus and the lists of names in 1 Chronicles. Every word that made it into the pages of Scripture is there on purpose.

The cool thing is that when we get into God's Word, it gets into us and produces amazing results. God's Word equips us for every good work!

When we get into God's Word, it gets
into us

Hopefully this makes you breathe a little lighter. God's Word is already all we need. It's not our job to make it something it's not. It's already relevant. The deeper you dig, the more relevance you'll uncover. Times and customs have changed, but people are basically the same. We struggle with the same issues and commit the same sins, they're just often warped, manipulated, and magnified by technology and advances of the modern age. People are people, whether they're living with Jesus or thousands of years after He walked the earth.

The same words God spoke to them are applicable and relevant to us today.

PAY ATTENTION!

As Peter describes the process of revelation and the penning of the words of Scripture, he says, "you will do well to pay attention as to a lamp shining in a dark place (2 Peter 1:19 ESV)."

I love his straightforward approach here: "You will do well to pay attention." Don't nod off, drift off, or goof off. Straighten up, listen up, and look up. We need to pay attention to God's Word and its relevance to our lives, churches, and culture.

Here's how we say it at Awaken:

God's Word defines us. Awaken Church is founded on, shaped by, and focused on the exposition of God's Word. We believe God's Word is alive and active and will preach it as such, regardless of whom it offends.

And speaking of offending people, you can count on God's Word doing that. I've had people walk out while I'm preaching, once as I warned people that the topic we would be discussing in Song of Solomon was a bit erotic, to say the least. Another time, a guy walked out after I read a few verses from 1 Timothy that deal with homosexuality (as well as many other things). I found out later he is gay and was offended immediately just by what the Bible had to say. I was sad he left because he never got to hear the loving approach I took on the topic. We don't set out to offend people, in fact, we go to great lengths not to offend people...unless it's with the gospel.

We want people's experience at church to be warm, welcoming, inviting, and comfortable from the moment their tires hit the pavement of our parking lot. From the verbiage and paint colors we use to the modern design and media, we try to make sure the whole experience is enjoyable. We pay close attention to everything from the parking experience to visitors, Awaken Kids, and even our coffee, restrooms, seating, music, and so much more. If you think that stuff doesn't matter to God, you haven't read much of the Old Testament where God details for dozens of chapters exactly what He wants the tabernacle and temple to look like. He cares about the details, all the way down to the fabric type and color as well as the pattern and colors of thread. He was extremely specific with the ornate details of the temple, the priests' clothing, and ceremonial worship experiences.

If we're going to offend someone, we want it to be because of the loving truths of God's Word that we spoke into their lives.

"

If we're going to offend someone, we want it to be because of the loving truths of God's Word that we spoke into their lives.

PUT YOUR OXYGEN MASK ON

Depending on how often you fly, you may be able to do the airline safety demonstration from memory.

The nearest exit may be behind you...

Floatation devices are under your seats...

Seat belts buckle like they have since they were first created...

That all makes sense. It's the part about the oxygen masks that always seemed so illogical to me. Essentially, they're telling me that if I'm traveling with my kids and the cabin pressure changes so suddenly that it shoots oxygen masks out of the overhead compartment, I'm supposed to calmly grab mine first and put it on while my kids are panicked, crying, and potentially gasping for air? Not only does this go against logic and my natural parental protective nature, but it seems selfish and wrong. Doesn't caring for my kids require self-sacrifice? That's what my sleep habits told me when we began having kids. Sleeping till 11:00 am on a Saturday was nice and all, but that waved goodbye the moment our first adorable, tiny, screaming human came home from the hospital in 2006. Since then, life has been about sacrificing myself for my kids. Jenn and I sacrifice sleep, money, a quiet house, and sometimes our sanity for those amazing little mini-mes. So why should that change when I board an airplane and endure a level of turbulence so jarring and uncomfortable that it results in me awkwardly breathing through a yellow plastic mask attached to a bag of air (which, according to the safety briefing, may or may not inflate)?

The answer is simple: A pile of dad in the aisle is of no assistance. I cannot help my kids if I'm passed out on the floor.

In other words, for their own health and safety, I need to take care of myself. In order for me to care for them, I must care for myself. This is one reason why, when you hear someone recall a life-threatening experience they went through, they often mention that they just wanted to make it home to their kids. Not only do they love their kids, but they know so much of their kids' survival is tied to their own survival and well-being.

The same is true spiritually. As selfish or illogical as it may sound, understand that as a leader, the spiritual health of those you lead is often deeply and directly impacted by your spiritual health. If you're not spiritually healthy, how will you lead them to be? If you're a burned out mess, how will you lead your church in spiritual life and growth? This is why our church has paid for months of counseling for my wife and I. Whether we were in a good season or a challenging one, our Board of Directors recognizes the importance of our mental and spiritual health and invests into it. For Jenn and I, attending regular counseling is our mental health version of putting our oxygen mask on first.

Even more important than your mental health is your spiritual health. Calm down, counselors and mental health experts. I'm not saying mental health isn't important; I'm saying spiritual health is more important because it impacts the rest of who we are. Spiritual health deeply impacts mental health and even physical health. It's that important.

A church that is defined by God's Word must be led by leaders who are defined by God's Word. You can't lead your church to be spiritually healthy if you are not committed to maintaining your own spiritual health. You can put on a show for a while, but it won't last.

You can't lead your church to be spiritually healthy if you are not committed to maintaining your own spiritual health.

If you are defined by something, you are not defined by many other things. Being defined by God's Word means we are not defined by our experiences, our failures, our emotions, or the opinions of others. It means we take our direction, doctrine, and even our demeanor from God's Word.

So how do you do this? A life and ministry defined by God's

Word comes from a daily commitment to God's Word. Before Ezekiel could deliver God's message to Israel, God told him to eat the scroll (Ezekiel 3:1-3 ESV) and "receive in your heart, and hear with your ears (Ezekiel 3:10 ESV)." Before we can be messengers, we have to absorb the message. Do you make time to absorb the message before you preach it? Before you ever preach a message, you must receive that same message in your heart, believing in the power of God's Word and letting it transform your life. Don't just study the Bible to preach it to others. Study the Bible to live it for yourself. The loudest messages you ever preach will be with your life, not with a three-point outline and a catchy title.

"

Don't just study the Bible to preach it to others. Study the Bible to live it for yourself.

So what does it look like to have a church that is founded on, shaped by, and focused on God's Word? Let's work through each of those...

FOUNDED ON

Nashville, which is just forty minutes down the road from Clarksville is growing very quickly. Statistically, they say about one hundred people move there every day! That many people moving to the same city causes a rapid need for more buildings for people to live in. One of the best ways to fit lots of people into a tight space is to go high instead of wide, meaning the construction industry is booming in Nashville. There are days where I drive through Nashville and I can count twenty or thirty cranes just from a single spot on the Interstate. Watching the progress of the high rises is fascinating because the tallest buildings begin as giant holes in the ground. As I write, one high rise in particular is in its foundation phase, but currently, it's an entire city block that is a giant hole in the ground.

I've walked and driven by the giant city-block-size hole in the ground for months now and it seems like it's taking forever to get going on the real work. The problem is, if they skipped this step that seems to take forever and impede forward progress, it would endanger the longevity of the building and the lives of the people who step into it.

You can't go high unless you go deep. If you don't take your time in the foundation phase, making sure you're grounded in God's Word, the results can be disastrous. When it comes to church planting, if your foundation isn't firm and Biblical, you won't be able to withstand the storms that come your way. One fierce storm, one threatening situation, one financial issue could topple the whole thing if there's no foundation.

If you read this and begin to wonder if you even have a foundation at all, let me assure you that you do. Whether it's shaky or firm is another conversation, but there is a foundation in place. If you're in the pre-stages of your church right now, this is great timing. In fact, if you're nearing launch and realize your church will be founded on anything else besides God's Word (current trends or fads, selfish desires, a competitive or envious streak, etc.), pump the brakes now. Getting the foundation correct is worth a delayed launch. If the foundation is wrong, everything else will eventually shift and fall. You can't go high unless you go deep.

> If the foundation is wrong, everything else will eventually shift and fall. You can't go high unless you go deep.

If you've already launched your church or maybe you've taken a leadership position at a church and you realize it's not founded on God's Word, it's not too late. If you built a house before recognizing that the foundation was shifting, you would be out of luck. You would have to demolish the building and start from scratch. Not so with the church. Right now is the right time to build on the right foundation. Any sacrifice you need to make will be worth it in the long run. Similar to how Jenn and I have taken couples through "pre-marital" counseling post-marriage, it's never too late to make some strategic shifts that will lay a firm foundation that was never laid or that you drifted from.

Building on a firm foundation is biblical. Jesus told a story about two men who built on different foundations: rock and sand. You can guess which one survived the storm. He compared the wisdom of the man who built on the rock with the wisdom of those who follow and obey His commands.

Speaking of foundations, Jesus Himself is referred to as the chief cornerstone. To this day, the cornerstone of a building is its most important stone. It is the first stone set in the construction of the foundation of a building. Its presence and placement are extremely important because all other stones are set in reference to this one stone. The position of the entire structure is based on the placement of this one stone. In 2 Peter 2, Peter reminds us that Jesus is that stone! The lives we live and the churches we lead should find their strength and bearing from the Chief Cornerstone, Jesus.

The early church faced a critical juncture in Acts 6. There was some tension in the church and some of the Hellenistic Jews felt as though their widows were being overlooked in the daily distribution of food. Although the church leaders may not have grasped the full gravity of the moment, I believe in many ways this was a hinge point for the church. The needs of the widows were important, but they were not foundational. A church built on meeting the needs of people instead of teaching the Word of God isn't a church, it's a social club. We have plenty of those. As church leaders, one of our main roles is to keep the main thing the main thing. Since the cornerstone is by definition the main thing, for the life of our churches, we will need to fight to keep it the main thing. Thankfully the early church leaders chose wisely. They appointed leaders to take care of the needs of those in the church and told them, "We will devote ourselves to prayer and to the ministry of the word." Had they chosen to abandon those, it would have been detrimental to the future of the church. If you choose to abandon prayer and the ministry of the word in order to please people, turn your resignation in now and go run a family fun center. You have a bright future with bumper cars and skee-ball.

Here are a few questions you can ask yourself and/or your team to assess the strength of your foundation:

When we are unsure or fearful, who or what do we turn to first?
When things aren't going as we planned, how do we tend to respond?
How do we gauge success?

SHAPED BY

I'm not a gardener and I do not have a green thumb. The Miller house is a place where plants come to die. Kevin Kölsch directed the movie *Pet Sematary* and Kevin Miller has a plant cemetery. I imagine we have a reputation in the botany community.

Although I don't garden, God spoke to me through some gardening once as I went through a tough season in ministry. One Saturday, I received an angry email from a long-time friend of mine who chose to leave the church in a very divisive way...via email. We were already dealing with a few similar, yet disconnected situations, and I was fed up. For some reason, I figured I would do some gardening. Everything else felt out of control, but I could control some freaking rose bushes and shrubbery! We had some irises in the front of our house that I didn't know how to prune, so I figured I'd watch a YouTube tutorial on it. I found a video and watched as the on-screen gardener talked to me about the importance of regular pruning. He said you have to cut the shoots down low and get the dead and dying leaves out. He mentioned that regular pruning prevents decay and disease and it helps promote the growth of the plant. As I cut the shoots, I kept thinking, "This does not feel like it will help this plant grow. It feels counter-productive, actually."

Suddenly it hit me. The guy in the YouTube video may have just been sharing some gardening tips, but God was using him to share some spiritual growth tips to a hurting pastor. In that moment, I realized I was in a season of feeling the pain of pruning. God was shaping me and shaping our church. As I stood for biblical doctrine and fought for unity, some people weren't going to understand or stick around. They needed to be weeded out. Maybe for their health or maybe for my health or the church's. Either way, I remembered in that moment that pruning, although painful, is profitable. Just like shaping an arrow requires cutting pieces away, allowing God to shape me and our church requires some painful surgery at times. But like that arrow, we'll be sharper and fly further once we're shaped.

> **"I am the true vine, and my Father is the vinedresser. Every branch in me that does not bear fruit he takes away, and every branch that does bear fruit he prunes, that it may bear more fruit."**
> **(John 15:1-2 ESV)**

Did you catch that last line? "...that it may bear more fruit."

The whole purpose of allowing God's Word to shape us is for our growth, not our death.

He's not just working despite the pain;
He's working with and through the
pain. He may not have caused the
pain, but He will use the pain.

Nobody ever said pruning was painless. Even Mr. Plant Killer over here knows that. In fact, not only does pruning involve pain, but in the middle of it, it sometimes looks and feels less like growth and more like death. I get it. We've been through seasons in the first ten years of our church where attendance dropped, giving was down, and the list of people who had issues they wanted to meet with me about seemed endless. But in the waiting and through the weeding, God is working. In fact, He's not just working despite the pain; He's working with and through the pain. He may not have caused the pain, but He will use the pain. That's the beautiful thing about being the Redeemer. Anything can be turned around and put to work for good.

Being founded on God's Word is a one time thing. You can change your foundation, but your life is only built on one main thing at a time. On the other hand, being shaped by God's Word is ongoing.

Where do you get your direction from?

God will show you where to go and what to do as you continue to seek Him.

FOCUSED ON

INTJ. That's my personality type, according to the Myers-Briggs personality assessment.

On the Enneagram, I'm an eight and partly a seven.

I don't know my zodiac sign, nor do I care to.

I also don't know my spirit animal, although my daughter says hers is the llama.

Those are just some of the latest personality and StrengthsFinder assessments to hit mainstream pop culture. In a quest to understand our idiosyncrises, thought patterns, and social habits, many people turn to these assessments. The typical response is, "I'm a _____ (fill in personality type), so no wonder I _____ (fill in habit, method, or response)." Those can be very helpful assessments and tools for leadership and life in general. However, we can't allow them to define and direct our lives.

In Jesus' day, the Jews were known by a different personality type. It wasn't ISFJ or ENTJ, it was POTB. The Jews were known as People Of The Book. Focusing on the Word of God was so ingrained in who they were that it became part of how they were known!

Although being "shaped by" God's Word requires allowing God to shape us, it's somewhat passive. It's something that happens to us as a result of being founded on God's Word. Being focused on God's Word is different though. It's active. It requires a personal pursuit. Just like knowing your personality type requires research and investment, so does being focused on God's Word. It requires a lifetime of research and investment, pouring yourself into God's Word and allowing it to pour into you.

This pursuit of God's Word reminds me of the Christians who lived in Berea in Acts 17. As Paul made his way through their region, Luke, the author of Acts tells us the Bereans were "examining the Scriptures daily to see if these things were so." They weren't going to just believe something because a preacher said it. I hope the same will be said of us. We don't believe things simply because someone who claims to speak for God said it. We don't practice it simply because everyone else is doing it. We don't implement that new idea simply because it worked for that guy or that church or that conference. If we are going to be people of the Book, we must give our lives to be focused on the Book.

For a few years, a couple professional bodybuilders came to our church. Early in their marriage, they had both won national championships, and they still look the part. Somehow I ended up with a gym membership at the same gym they went to, so naturally I asked him to show me around a bit. Show me he did! He would sit down at the chest press or lie down at the leg press, do some rows or cable crossovers to demonstrate, then have me do the same. I pushed through it at first, but partway through, I told him I needed to sit down for a minute. I felt light-headed and nauseated.

At the time, going to the gym was a thing I did periodically when I felt particularly motivated or out of shape. For Josh, the gym was life. Everyone knew him and he knew every machine. And you should see his home gym! At one point as he was showing me around at the gym, his wife, who has bigger biceps than most people I know, walked up to us. Dripping sweat, clearly ready to be done with her workout, she spoke some words of discouragement into my life that day. "After years and years of working out, it never gets any easier," she told me. "Gee, thanks," I thought. Can't wait!

Here's the hard truth: you don't get biceps the size of my waist on accident. It requires a purposeful pursuit. Technology has brought us a long way, but we have yet to figure out a way to have someone else go to the gym for us while we reap the benefits. Physical health requires a personal, purposeful pursuit. The same is true spiritually. Whenever you meet someone who knows God's Word well or prays powerfully, remember that didn't happen by accident. It took years of intentionality to get to that point, and it will take the rest of their lives to continue to grow.

What I called "going to the gym," he called "training." Cardio and weights is just what Josh did. It wasn't a pastime or a hobby. It was a routine part of his life. It reminds me of what Paul told Timothy:

> **"...train yourself for godliness; for while bodily training is of some value, godliness is of value in every way, as it holds promise for the present life and also for the life to come."**
> **(1 Timothy 4:7-8 ESV)**

You won't wake up one day and realize you have a godly life. Instead, it requires the ongoing, intentional discipline of focusing on God's Word

In the original language, that word "train" has sweat all over it. It's a throbbing, sweaty mess of a word that describes a purposeful pursuit of godliness. It comes with the understanding that you won't wake up one day and realize you have a godly life. Instead, it requires the ongoing, intentional discipline of focusing on

God's Word, knowing that "it holds promise for the present life and also for the life to come."

Our belief in the power of God's Word produces an unapologetic approach to how we handle it and prioritize it in the churches we lead and lives we invest in.

We've spent the first decade of our church taking old buildings and spaces and making them relevant to fit our needs today. That's our approach with buildings, and although the Bible is relevant already, it still takes work to teach it in a relevant, applicable way.

I think sometimes the church is guilty of answering questions no one is asking. While we're over here discussing the potential identities of Gog and Magog, the two witnesses in Revelation, and parsing Greek verbs, the people sitting in our churches are wondering how their three-year-old is going to survive the cancer diagnosis they just received and someone else is terrified of what will happen if their marriage doesn't survive. There is certainly a time and a place to answer the questions about apocalyptic prophecy and original languages, but let's not neglect the glaring, life-altering, practical needs that impact the daily lives and relationships of the people who make up our churches.

Paul gave Timothy a lot of leadership and pastoral advice. 1 and 2 Timothy are absolute pastoral gold mines. From church leadership to facing false teachers, stewarding finances to prioritizing prayer, the roles of men and women in the church to spiritual gifts... Virtually everything you need to know about leading the local church is found in those two letters. Out of it all, one gem shines above the rest, and it's only three words:

"Preach the word."
(2 Timothy 4:2 ESV)

There are many other things pastors can and should do, but this is a non-negotiable. In fact, if you get everything else right, but you miss this, you miss it all.

HUGS AND TRUTH

I always love hearing specific ways a message I've given impacts people. By far, the thing I get thanked for the most is my willingness to speak hard, honest truths (in love). The world has plenty of entertainment, thrills, and feel-good experiences. What they need is truth. I'm not saying church shouldn't be fun. Church should be *enjoyed*, not *endured*. While we should never use truth to beat people up or guilt them into something, I am saying not to avoid truth. Paul and Timothy didn't avoid it, and neither did Jesus.

"But it just doesn't seem very loving," people will say. There are certainly plenty of preachers who speak the truth, but in very harsh, abrasive, demeaning ways. You may have seen YouTube clips of preachers climbing on their pulpit, screaming demeaning names at the people in the pews, and even using racial slurs to get their point across. That's the opposite of what God wants. Speak the truth in love and let God do the heart convicting and soul changing.

Also, who said truth wasn't loving? A big mud and rock slide recently blocked all of I-24 East heading into Nashville. The most loving, helpful thing they can do is tell us the truth: it's dangerous to proceed - go a different route!

Don't apologize for God's Word.

Jesus wasn't scared to say it how it is. Read John 6 when Jesus told the massive crowd that they had to eat His flesh and drink His blood. I'll bet even the disciples were disappointed when that came flying out of Jesus' mouth. "We had finally gathered a big crowd and then Jesus goes into the blood and body bit!"

You are not God's PR rep, trying to make Him appealing to the masses. He doesn't need your help with marketing, and He certainly doesn't want you apologizing on His behalf for the hard truths of Scripture. He included the tough stuff for a reason. Speak it in love, live it yourself, commit to walking it out with people, and let God take care of the results.

He included the tough stuff for a
reason. Speak it in love, live it yourself,
commit to walking it out with people,
and let God take care of the results.

And by the way, although you should never set out to offend people, if you're going to offend someone, offend them with truth.

Don't let a non-essential side issue be the thing that ticks them off and makes them leave.

And while you're at it, remember that there's a big difference between teaching the Bible and teaching about the Bible.

A lot of pastors teach *about* the Bible. It's challenging to find pastors who teach the Bible.

Teaching *about* the Bible often involves using the Bible to prove your point or drive home your idea. In this case, the Bible is more of a crutch you lean on or a step stool to help you onto your soap box.

Teaching the Bible means letting Scripture lead the way. In this case, the Bible isn't a crutch that supports your ideas, it's the foundation and the framework that supports the whole structure.

God's Word is God-breathed. Let it loose and let it do its thing in the lives of those you preach to! Charles Spurgeon said, "Defend the Bible? I would as soon defend a lion! Unchain it and it will defend itself."

UNTIL EVERYONE KNOWS JESUS

As leaders of the Church and ambassadors of Christ, Jesus has left us with a staggering and sobering responsibility: taking the gospel to the ends of the earth.

Carrying the message of the cross to a lost and dying world is an unbelievable privilege and a weighty opportunity. Whether we rise to meet Jesus in the air or our lungs take their final breath on earth and their next breath in heaven, the day will come when we stand face to face with Jesus. Although heaven will be a beautiful place of unbelievable joy, that staggering, sobering responsibility and opportunity to deliver the life-changing message of the gospel will forever be gone. Although we will rejoice in the presence of Jesus, we will no longer have the privilege of speaking the gospel and watching it transform a life. When we wake up in Jesus' presence, our days of evangelism will be a thing of the past.

This is why our message is so urgent.

This is why Paul exhorts Timothy not to get distracted by ancillary arguments or distracting discourses.

Taking the gospel to the ends of the earth is what we are called to give our lives for.

If you will be still and listen, you'll begin to see that the pages of your Bible have a pulse. Jesus is the heartbeat of Scripture. He's the seed of the woman in Genesis, the Passover lamb in Exodus, the High Priest in Leviticus, the water and bread in the desert in Numbers, the prophet like Moses in Deuteronomy, and His pulse is pounding throughout the other sixty-one books of the Bible as well. If you cut the Bible, it bleeds Jesus. The Bible isn't just a collection of stories; it is THE story.

Since Jesus' love is the heartbeat of Scripture, that same love must be the heartbeat of our lives and our churches.

Take a deep breath. Are your lungs still inhaling and exhaling? As long as Jesus hasn't returned yet and our lungs still have breath in them, we refuse to sit back, slow down, or give up. We will keep going until every person knows Jesus or we die trying, come hell or high water.

EPILOGUE

My pen pal is in prison.

He has been since 1998 when he was convicted of murder. In a tragic case of mistaken vigilante justice, he targeted a man in a daycare parking lot and fired a semiautomatic weapon through the man's driver side door. Forty-year old Paul Wong died the following day of multiple gunshot wounds. Bryan Modglin was arrested shortly afterward, receiving a sentence of twenty-five years to life in prison. [1]

That turn of events changed his life in more ways than one.

Behind prison bars, Bryan put his faith in Jesus, changing his eternal destination and the trajectory of his life.

In 2010, Bryan began taking online courses from Calvary Chapel Bible College (CCBC), the time Bryan says marked the period of his greatest spiritual growth. Prior to graduating in 2017, one of his final classes was Church Planting 101, a two-week block course I taught at CCBC in 2013.

Bryan wrote:

"I took Pastor Kevin's Church Planting class and he quickly became my hero as I listened to his lectures over and over. God had already used him to do exactly what I dreamed of. Because of his transparency I reached out to him thinking maybe he'd be willing to invest in my life...He has been a steady source of wisdom and support as God uses me to lead the guys in here...For over twenty years, I've been pouring myself into the lives of those around me. If granted parole my desire is to use all I've learned from Pastor Kevin to plant a church in Arkansas and invest myself in those whom the Lord brings near. The number one lesson I stand on is to trust and rely on the Lord and not our abilities or strength. My prayer is His will be done."

God specializes in using the most unexpected people to do the most unbelievable things. He has been doing it for thousands of years:

Moses, the murderer turned rescuer of Israel...
Rahab, the prostitute turned spy protector...
David, the shepherd turned giant slayer...
Mary Magdalene, the demoniac turned evangelist...

Saul of Tarsus, the Christian killer turned Christ preacher and church planter...
Peter...
James...
Judas...
Bryan Modglin...
Kevin Miller...

God used some pretty gnarly people to build His church.

For Jesus to build a team while He was on earth, then hand them the keys to the Church to continue building what He had founded, you would think He would choose the all-stars. The A-team. The Navy Seals of church planting: specially trained, sophistically dressed, and socially superior. This would be a highly elite team that even the best wouldn't measure up to. These would be the best of the best.

Whoever was on this team of world-changers, you definitely wouldn't include a rowdy, rag-tag group of mostly teenage boys, rejected by the other Jewish rabbis, on the fringes of society, with criminal pasts, mouths like sailors, and a constant nack for bickering, backstabbing, and betrayal. And at the very least, you wouldn't knowingly choose a guy who would betray you in the future. Nobody does that.

Unless you're Jesus.

In that case, you do all of that, and many, many more illogical, against-common-sense-and-everything-your-marketing-professor-taught-you ideas. I guess when You are the Son of God incarnate you can do what you want. His choice of these men and women throughout history was not a flippant decision or a passive aggressive method of rebellion. It was a prayerful (as in twelve hours through the night), careful decision as well as a pattern for the future.

Had He chosen only the elite, He would have alienated the 99.9% of the rest of us that wouldn't classify ourselves as such. You and I would never have made the cut.

In many ways, the story of Awaken Church is an anomaly. There are many reasons what we did shouldn't have worked. From the lack of training to begin with to the burgers at parks marketing scheme, from the flood to the financial issues and overall inexperience. The reality is, I relate a lot more to Peter than I'd like to admit. I've put my foot in my mouth many times, and although I have yet to chop a guy's ear off with a sword, I have at times been known to arrogantly and/or angrily take swings at people I should have prayed for instead.

People have asked if I would redo our church plant if I could. My response is always no. Although we will do it differently in the future, I wouldn't change a thing from the past. God has a way of using all of my inconsistencies, failures, and inexperience for His glory and my good.

Don't count yourself out and don't count anyone else out.

If God could use Rahab, Peter, Mary, Bryan, me, and a host of other unexpected, uneducated, unknown people to build His Church and change the world, God can use you and the person you think He is least likely to use. So grab that list of people you think God could never use, then find the nearest paper shredder and feed it some lunch.

Come hell or high water, let's stop at nothing to build The Church. If Jesus died to build it, it only makes sense that we would give our lives to do the same thing.

ACKNOWLEDGEMENTS

Jenn: Thank you for following me into this wild ride and being so constant even through the times when everything else is chaotic.

Tiffany: Thanks for working so incredibly hard behind the scenes to bring this book to life. I couldn't have done this without your hard work and persistence.

Kara: Thanks for reading, editing, and helping see my writing from a different perspective.

Quent: Your expert feedback and critique were not only helpful, but also more encouraging than you know. Plus, you read and edited the book in six days! You're a beast!

Jason: Thanks for believing in this project and for making space and time to help record and edit the audio book.

Tina: Thanks for finding all of the great locations around Nashville for me to write.

Nate, Jenn, and Denver: Thanks for following us to Clarksville and joining us for this wild adventure of church planting.

Renee: Thanks for publishing months of church planting blogs and emails, helping me lay the groundwork for this book.

Ellie: The artwork is ridiculous. Thanks for your skills and hard work. I hope you didn't take your frustration out on Grant too hard!

Richard: That photo on the back of the book...daaaang! Thanks for the shots!

Mom: Thanks for faithfully praying for more than a decade now. So much of the power of our ministry is fruit to your account.

Tim: Thanks for lending your skills for the book trailer. It's even better than I saw it in my head!

Awaken Church: It is one of the greatest honors of my life to lead and serve alongside such incredible people.

To the thousands of people who have prayed, given, encouraged, and supported us and Awaken Church through the years, **THANK YOU!** We are so grateful.

To the people below (including the anonymous ones not named) who supported this book through GoFundMe before you even knew the title or much of what it was about: Thank you for catching the vision and investing in it!

Darren Anderson

Stephen & Julia Arnold

Jebiemil Banal

Drew Bentley

Lorin Bentley

Biblical Merch

Cathy Boles

Hampton Bourne

Joshua & Ricketta Brimmer

Joseph Byl

Alicia Castillo

Butch & Vickie Clark

Sam & Degee Cruz-Roberts

Krista Davis

Andy Deane

Isaac & Courtney Del Toro

Tiago & Kara De Oliveira

Pamela Dill

Crystal Dozier

Karla Duitman

Josh & DeNicka Edwards

Michael & Ellen Emrick

Josh Hedberg

Gina & Jon Fox

Keith Gallo

Jackie Garrett

Joe & Yvette Gutierrez

Jennifer Harper

Eric & Kelly Harrison

Vince & Yvette Harrison

Charles Hudlin

Debbie & Brian Keele

AJ & Breezy Krueger

Carl Livingston

Aliza & Cesar Loya

Luke MacDonald

Sarah Magee

Eric Martinez

April McAlpin

Charles & Kristina Metge

Dennis & Melissa Miller

Jessica Moore

Aaron Mose

Sarah Mosso

Ruben Ortiz

Kelsey Palmer

Ethan Reimann

Rebekah Rendon

Renee Robins

Greg & Debbie Rockhold

Paul Rockhold

Tiffany Rockhold

Jason & Cortni Roy

Rachael Rundall

Carlo Serrano

The Sheppard's

The Snipes Family

Josh Sorensen

Mike Sternad

Ashley & Ryan Upton

Tommy Vallejos

Nelson and Trisha Walker

Chris Ward

Tim and Tina Medina

Brittany & Zack Wendell

Jordee Wester

Kristina Williams

Shawna Willis

Nate & Jenn Witiuk

Freddy T. Wyatt

Ryan & Natalie Wylie

NOTES

Chapter 1, Don't Jump Until You're Ready
1. "List of hobbies," in Wikipedia, August 21, 2019 https://en.wikipedia.org/wiki/List_of_hobbies
2. C.H. Spurgeon, Lectures to My Students, Complete & Unabridged, published by Zondervan.

Chapter 2, Operation: Location Determination
1. The National Map Small Scale. USGS. 2018. https://nationalmap.gov/small_scale/mld/citiesx.html
2. Mark Batterson, The Circle Maker, published by Zondervan, 2011.

Chapter 5, Bye Bye, Mike Wazowski
1. Houston, Brian (@BrianCHouston). "Hillsong church is not built on the gifts and talents of a few, but on the sacrifices of many!"
October 26, 2015, 11:31 AM. https://mobile.twitter.com/brianchouston/status/658682411748712448

Chapter 7, Spot Lights and Stab Wounds
1. Allyson Chiu,"'She seems to have crushed his throat': Lioness at zoo kills father of her cubs in 'unprovoked' attack," The Washington Post, October 22, 2018 https://www.washingtonpost.com/nation/2018/10/22/she-seems-have-crushed-his-throat-lioness-indianapolis-zoo-kills-father-cubs-unprovoked-attack/

Epilogue
1. The Associated Press, "Ex-Wife, 2 Others Held In Fatal Shooting," Los Angeles Times, September 18, 1998, https://www.latimes.com/archives/la-xpm-1998-sep-18-me-24072-story.html

Made in the USA
Las Vegas, NV
01 July 2022

50971866R00118